International Labour and Employment Compliance Handbook

www.kluwerlawonline.com

Labour and Employment Compliance in Poland

International Bar Association

Labour and Employment Compliance in Poland

Tenth Edition

Barbara Jozwik

This publication is part of the International Labour and Employment Compliance Handbook, available on www.kluwerlawonline.com

Editors: Salvador del Rey and Robert J. Mignin
Associate Editor: Juan Bonilla

INTERNATIONAL BAR ASSOCIATION
the global voice of the legal profession

Wolters Kluwer

Published by:
Kluwer Law International B.V.
PO Box 316
2400 AH Alphen aan den Rijn
The Netherlands
E-mail: lrs-sales@wolterskluwer.com
Website: www.wolterskluwer.com/en/solutions/kluwerlawinternational

Sold and distributed by:
Wolters Kluwer Legal & Regulatory U.S.
7201 McKinney Circle
Frederick, MD 21704
United States of America
E-mail: customer.service@wolterskluwer.com

ISBN 978-94-035-0316-5

e-Book: ISBN 978-94-035-0616-6
web-PDF: ISBN 978-94-035-0626-5

All listed titles are also available on lrus.wolterskluwer.com

1. Argentina: Julio César Stefanoni Zani & Enrique Alfredo Betemps, *Labour and Employment Compliance in Argentina, 10th edition*, 2022 (ISBN 978-94-035-4332-1)
2. Australia: John Tuck, Stephen Price, Rosemary Roach, Jack de Flamingh, Nicholas Ellery & Nick Le Mare, *Labour and Employment Compliance in Australia, 6th edition*, 2021 (ISBN 978-94-035-3914-0)
3. Belgium: Chris Van Olmen, *Labour and Employment Compliance in Belgium, 7th edition*, 2022 (ISBN 978-94-035-4374-1)
4. Brazil: Rodrigo Seizo Takano, Andrea Giamondo Massei & Murilo Caldeira Germiniani, *Labour and Employment Compliance in Brazil, 9th edition*, 2022 (ISBN 978-94-035-4991-0)
5. Canada: Kevin Coon & Adrian Ishak, *Labour and Employment Compliance in Canada, 2nd edition*, 2014 (ISBN 978-90-411-5637-2)
6. Chile: Gerardo Otero A., María Dolores Echeverría F., María de los Ángeles Fernández S. & Javier Sabido, *Labour and Employment Compliance in Chile, 10th edition*, 2022 (ISBN 978-94-035-4404-5)
7. China: King & Wood Mallesons, *Labour and Employment Compliance in China, 6th edition*, 2021 (ISBN 978-94-035-3894-5)
8. France: Pascale Lagesse, *Labour and Employment Compliance in France, 10th edition*, 2022 (ISBN 978-94-035-4384-0)
9. Germany: Gerlind Wisskirchen & Martin Lützeler, *Labour and Employment Compliance in Germany, 10th edition*, 2022 (ISBN 978-94-035-4454-0)
10. India: Manishi Pathak, *Labour and Employment Compliance in India, 10th edition*, 2022 (ISBN 978-94-035-4362-8)
11. Ireland: Duncan Inverarity & Ailbhe Dennehy, *Labour and Employment Compliance in Ireland, 9th edition*, 2022 (ISBN 978-94-035-0326-4)
12. Israel: Pnina Broder-Manor, Helen Raziel & Ilan Winder, *Labour and Employment Compliance in Israel, 9th edition*, 2022 (ISBN 978-94-035-4424-3)
13. Italy: Angelo Zambelli, *Labour and Employment Compliance in Italy, 10th edition*, 2022 (ISBN 978-94-035-4372-7)
14. Japan: Yoshikazu Sugino, *Labour and Employment Compliance in Japan, 10th edition*, 2022 (ISBN 978-94-035-4342-0)
15. Republic of Korea: Sang Wook Cho, Soojung Lee & Christopher Mandel, *Labour and Employment Compliance in the Republic of Korea, 8th edition*, 2022 (ISBN 978-94-035-4434-2)
16. Mexico: Oscar De La Vega Gómez, *Labour and Employment Compliance in Mexico, 10th edition*, 2022 (ISBN 978-94-035-4414-4)
17. The Netherlands: Els de Wind & Cara Pronk, *Labour and Employment Compliance in the Netherlands, 5th edition*, 2022 (ISBN 978-94-035-1594-6)
18. Poland: Barbara Jóźwik, *Labour and Employment Compliance in Poland, 10th edition*, 2022 (ISBN 978-94-035-0316-5)
19. Russia: Anna-Stefaniya Chepik, *Labour and Employment Compliance in Russia*, 2013 (ISBN 978-90-411-4925-1)

20. Saudi Arabia: Sara Khoja & Sarit Thomas, *Labour and Employment Compliance in Saudi Arabia, 5th edition,* 2022 (ISBN 978-94-035-4394-9)
21. South Africa: Susan Stelzner, Stuart Harrison, Brian Patterson & Zahida Ebrahim, *Labour and Employment Compliance in South Africa, 10th edition*, 2022 (ISBN 978-94-035-4474-8)
22. Spain: Salvador del Rey, Ana Campos & Sergi Gálvez Duran, *Labour and Employment Compliance in Spain, 10th edition*, 2022 (978-94-035-4352-9)
23. Turkey: Sertaç Kökenek & Elif Nur Çakır Vurgun, *Labour and Employment Compliance in Turkey, 8th edition*, 2022 (ISBN 978-94-035-0336-3)
24. United Arab Emirates: Sara Khoja & Sarit Thomas, *Labour and Employment Compliance in the United Arab Emirates, 9th edition*, 2022 (ISBN 978-94-035-4444-1)
25. United Kingdom: Ed Mills, Ailie Murray, Anna West, Gareth Walls, Emmie Ellison & Elliot English, *Labour and Employment Compliance in The United Kingdom, 3rd edition*, 2022 (ISBN 978-94-035-4464-9)
26. United States: Andrew J. Boling, Amy de La Lama, William Dugan, Chris Guldberg, Brian Hengesbaugh, Robert J. Mignin, Virginia Mohr, John M. Murphy & Ginger Partee, *Labour and Employment Compliance in the United States, 7th edition*, 2022 (ISBN 978-94-035-3921-8)

International Bar Association
The Global Voice of the Legal Profession

The International Bar Association (IBA), established in 1947, is the world's leading organization of international legal practitioners, bar associations and law societies. The IBA influences the development of international law reform and shapes the future of the legal profession throughout the world. It has a membership of over 40,000 individual lawyers and almost 200 bar associations and law societies spanning all continents. It has considerable expertise in providing assistance to the global legal community.

Grouped into two divisions – the Legal Practice Division and the Public and Professional Interest Division – the IBA covers all practice areas and professional interests, providing members with access to leading experts and up-to-date information. Through the various committees of the divisions, the IBA enables an interchange of information and views among its members as to laws, practices and professional responsibilities relating to the practice of business law around the globe. Additionally, the IBA's high-quality publications and world-class conferences provide unrivalled professional development and network-building opportunities for international legal practitioners and professional associates.

The IBA's Bar Issues Commission provides an invaluable forum for IBA member organisations to discuss all matters relating to law at an international level.

The IBA's Human Rights Institute (IBAHRI) works across the Association, to promote, protect and enforce human rights under a just rule of law, and to preserve the independence of the judiciary and the legal profession worldwide.

Other institutions established by the IBA include the Southern Africa Litigation Centre and the International Legal Assistance Consortium.

Employment and Industrial Relations Law Committee

The aims of the committee are to develop and exchange knowledge of employment and industrial relations law and practice. Members support each other through the provision of innovative ideas and practical assistance on day-to-day issues. In addition, through its journal and through presentations, conferences, the committee ensures the dissemination of up-to-date law and practice in this highly important business area.

International Bar Association Global Employment Institute

The IBA Global Employment Institute (IBA GEI) was formed in early 2010 for the purpose of developing for multinationals and worldwide institutions a global and strategic approach to the key legal issues in the human resources and human capital fields.

Drawing on the resources and expertise of the IBA membership, the IBA GEI will provide a unique contribution in the field of employment, discrimination and immigration law, on a diverse range of global issues, to private and public organizations throughout the world. The IBA GEI is designed to enhance the management, performance and productivity of these organizations and help achieve best practice in their human capital and management functions from a strategic perspective.

The IBA GEI will become the leading voice and authority on global HR issues by virtue of having a number of the world's leading labour and employment practitioners in its ranks, and the support and resource of the world's largest association of international lawyers.

Further information

International Bar Association, 4th Floor, 10 St Bride Street, London EC4A 4AD, United Kingdom, Tel: +44 (0)20 7842 0090, Fax: +44 (0)20 7842 0091, E-mail: member@int-bar.org, www.ibanet.org

About the International Labour and Employment Compliance Handbook

From 1976 through 1988, the International Bar Association and Kluwer Law International published the groundbreaking International Handbook on Contracts of Employment. This Handbook provided one of the first global overviews of the law of the international employment relationship.

Since publishing the first edition, globalization of business has created an increased demand for knowledge of labor and employment laws throughout the world. Therefore, along with Kluwer, we decided to publish an updated Handbook which we have titled the International Labour and Employment Compliance Handbook.

This new Handbook was intended to be a practical guide by providing a general overview of key labor and employment issues in multiple jurisdictions. Each chapter was written so that it is easy to understand by lawyers and non-lawyers alike. Each country author has also followed a standard outline to assist readers in analysing employment issues in each country.

The first edition of this new Handbook included nineteen (19) different countries.

This Handbook would not have been possible without the help and assistance of many people. Most importantly, the individual country authors are all distinguished legal practitioners who spent considerable time drafting and revising their country reports to meet difficult deadlines. We thank each of them. Our friends at Kluwer, especially Ewa Szkatula, have done a wonderful job in keeping the editors and the authors on schedule. Finally, we want to also express our gratitude to Cuatrecasas, Gonçalves Pereira, and Baker & McKenzie LLP for their valuable assistance in the coordination and organization of this project. Our warmest thanks to each of them.

Because of the success of the Handbook,Wolters Kluwer Law & Business decided to publish each country report also as a separate book to give a choice in obtaining the information. We hope this new format will be a helpful and useful resource just like the Handbook. Both formats are available in print and online.

The Editors

Salvador del Rey Guanter
Robert J. Mignin

March 2013

Table of Contents

Poland

AUTHOR

Barbara Jóźwik

Barbara Jóźwik is an attorney at law and partner leading the employment practice of Schoenherr Warsaw. Schoenherr is a leading law firm in Central Europe with offices in Belgrade, Bratislava, Brussels, Bucharest, Budapest, Chisinau, Istanbul, Linz, Ljubljana, Podgorica, Prague, Sofia, Vienna, Warsaw and Zagreb. Barbara has more than twenty years of experience as an employment attorney. Barbara specializes in all aspects of employment law, including national and multi-jurisdictional issues, individual and collective employment law.

Barbara has particular experience in advising clients on drafting executive contracts, terminating contracts with top managers, drafting internal regulations, such as remuneration and working rules, and workplace bullying procedures, advising employers on such issues as employee incentive plans, bonus arrangements, restructuring and redundancies as well as negotiating settlements.

Her practice also includes negotiations with trade unions and works councils. She has experience with complex reorganizations and restructuring matters, including personnel reductions, works council/trade unions information/consultation requirements, harmonization of employee benefits, transfer of undertakings.

Barbara represents clients in labour courts. Most disputes concern not only mobbing and discrimination issues but also dismissals, overtime and remuneration, violation of non-competition contracts.

Previously, Barbara worked as an attorney at law in the law firm Gleiss Lutz (2004–2008) and Nörr Stiefenhofer Lutz (1998–2004) in Warsaw, where she also specialized in employment matters. Barbara is admitted to the Polish Bar Association (1998) and is a graduate of the University of Warsaw (German Philology and Law, Master's in 1991 and 1993). She is also a Member of the European Employment Lawyers Association and Europäischen Anwaltsvereinigung DACH.

Barbara is a frequent speaker at seminars on labour law. In addition, she is the author of various books and publications on labour law in the Polish business press.

ADDRESS

Schoenherr Attorneys at Law
PL-00-107 Warsaw
ul. Próżna 9
Tel.: +48 22 223 09 00
Fax: +48 22 223 09 02
E-mail: b.jozwik@schoenherr.eu
Web: www.schoenherr.eu

COVID-19 Information

Economic downtime

According to the COVID-19 regulations, an economic downtime could be introduced.

Conditions to be met include:

- decrease in economic turnover: (i) not less than 15%, calculated as the relation of total turnover over any two consecutive months in the period after 1 January 2020 to the total turnover from the corresponding two months of the previous year following the occurrence of COVID-19; or (ii) not less than 25%, calculated as the relation of total turnover during any freely indicated month in the period after 1 January 2020 compared to the turnover of the previous month;
- no tax arrears on account of contributions for social security, health insurance, the Labour Fund or the Fund by the end of the third quarter of 2019;
- salary: the employer must pay employees affected by the economic downtime at least 50% of their salaries, not less than PLN 3,010.00 (approx. EUR 640), considering their work time;
- exemption: high-salaried employees: the financing is not applicable to employees whose remuneration received in the month preceding the month in which the application was submitted was higher than PLN 17,985.27 (approx. EUR 4,050);
- prohibition of termination of employment contracts: maximum of three months of financing period;
- implementation: conclusion of an agreement with employee representatives required;
- co-financing: the fund will co-finance a maximum of 50% of the salary but no more than PLN 1,505.00 (approx. EUR 320) increased by social security contributions on this amount, considering employees' working time;

- period: due for a total period of three months, including the month of application.

Short-time working

According to the COVID-19 regulations, the employer is entitled to unilaterally reduce the working time.

Conditions to be met include:

- no grounds for declaring bankruptcy;– decrease in economic turnover: (i) not less than 15%, calculated as the relation of total turnover over any two consecutive months in the period after 1 January 2020 to the total turnover from the corresponding two months of the previous year following the occurrence of COVID-19; or (ii) not less than 25%, calculated as the relation of total turnover during any freely indicated month in the period after 1 January 2020 compared to the turnover of the previous month;
- no tax arrears on account of contributions for social security, health insurance, the Labour Fund or the Fund by the end of the third quarter of 2019;
- reducing working time by 20%, no more than half of full-time employment, subject to the remuneration not being lower than the minimum remuneration for work (PLN 3,010, approx. EUR 640), considering employee's working time;
- exemption: high-salaried employees: the financing is not applicable to employees whose remuneration received in the month preceding the month in which the application was submitted was higher than PLN 17,985.27 (approx. EUR 4,050);
- prohibition of termination of employment contracts: maximum of three months of financing period;
- implementation: conclusion of an agreement with employee representatives required;
- co-financing: the fund will co-finance a maximum of 40% of the average monthly remuneration from the previous quarter announced by the President of the Central Statistical Office, plus social security contributions due from the employer on the benefits granted, i.e., PLN 2,535.38 (approx. EUR 538). Employer's social security contributions from the granted compensation are paid from the Fund;
- period: due for a total period of three months, including the month of application.

Broader support for entrepreneurs

Apart from the above possibilities of introducing an economic downtime and unilaterally reducing the working time, the support for entrepreneurs has been broadened. An industry shield has been introduced for certain entrepreneurs currently most affected by the fall-winter wave of the COVID-19 pandemic, which provides assistance based on the Act on COVID-19 and regulations of the Council of Ministers.

The assistance provides for, among others:

- exemption from social security contributions;
- co-financing of employees' salaries.

The assistance applies to selected industries indicated by the regulations of the Council of Ministers after meeting certain conditions specified in the regulations – which change along with the duration of the COVID restrictions. Depending on the industry in which a given entrepreneur operates, due to its number of Polish classification of activities (*PKD*), it is possible to use all or some of the above-mentioned instruments.

Home-office

The new legislation enacted in response to the outbreak of the COVID crisis allows employers to order any employee employed to perform his/her work determined in the employment contract remotely. The employee's consent is not required.

According to the National Labour Inspectorate, an order to work from home can be given in any form, also verbally. However, employers should confirm an order to work from home in writing or in an official e-mail or, in the absence of other possibilities, by text message.

The remote work must be assigned for a specific period of time, although the regulations do not set either the minimum or maximum time. The length of time should be commensurate with the intended purpose, which is to prevent the spread of COVID-19. The period of remote work can be shortened or extended, so the employer is free to adjust it to the existing situation.

Conditions to be met in order to perform the remote work:

- the employee has the technical and local skills and capabilities to perform such work;
- the type of work allows it to be performed remotely.

The remote work may be performed with the use of means of direct remote communication or relate to the performance of manufacturing parts or material services.

Tools and materials needed to perform remote work and logistics support for remote work shall be provided by the employer. However, the employee may use other tools and materials (not provided by the employer) if it allows for the protection of confidential information and other legally protected secrets, including business secrets or personal data, as well as information the disclosure of which could harm the employer.

Moreover, at the employer's request, an employee performing the remote work is obliged to keep records of performed activities, considering a description of these activities, as well as the date and time of their performance (keeping such records is not obligatory).

Compulsory vacation leave

According to the new COVID-19 regulations, the employer may grant the employee a vacation leave not used by the employee in previous calendar years and the employee is obliged to use such leave. The employer makes such a decision unilaterally.

While sending the employee for the compulsory holiday leave, the employer does so:

– within the period specified by him;
– without the employee's consent, and
– disregarding the vacation plan.

Such compulsory holiday leave may cover a maximum of thirty days.

An equivalent working time system

The equivalent working time system introduced by the new legislation consists of extending the daily working time, but not more than twelve hours, in a settlement period not exceeding twelve months. Based on the Labour Code such an extension may only be made in a settlement period not exceeding one month and in particularly justified cases, the settlement period may be extended not more than up to three months. Thus, based on the new COVID-19 regulations the extension can take place in a settlement period not exceeding twelve months. It should be borne in mind that an extended daily working time shall be balanced by a shorter daily working time on certain days or days off work.

Conditions to be met include:

– decrease in economic turnover: (i) not less than 15%, calculated as the relation of total turnover over two consecutive months in the period after 1 January 2020 to the total turnover from the corresponding two months of the previous year following the occurrence of COVID-19 to the day preceding the day on which the employer decides to reduce uninterrupted

rest or to take action to conclude an agreement on less favourable conditions of employment; or (ii) not less than 25%, calculated as the relation of total turnover during any freely indicated month in the period after 1 January 2020–31 December 2019 to the day preceding the day on which the employer decides to reduce uninterrupted rest or to take action to conclude an agreement on less favourable conditions of employment, compared to the turnover of the previous month; or (iii) an increase in the quotient of the cost of remuneration of employees, including social security contributions of employees financed by the employer, and the revenue from the sale of goods or services from the same calendar month chosen by the entrepreneur from 1 March 2020 to the day preceding the day on which the employer decides to reduce uninterrupted rest or to take action to conclude an agreement on less favourable conditions of employment, by not less than 5% in comparison with such quotient of the turnover of the preceding month;
- no tax arrears on account of contributions for social security, health insurance, the Labour Fund or the Fund by the end of the third quarter of 2019.

The conclusion of an agreement on the introduction of an equivalent working time system based on the new COVID-19 regulations requires the employer's cooperation with trade unions or employees' representatives. Until now, under the Labour Code, if the employer was not covered by a collective labour agreement or was not obliged to establish work regulations, the employer could introduce a system of equivalent working time in the announcement. The current regulation in this case is a tightening of the code-related procedure.

Daily and weekly rest periods

The new COVID-19 regulations shortened the rest periods regulated by the Labour Code to not less than eight hours in case of daily rest and to not less than thirty-two hours of uninterrupted weekly rest, including at least eight hours of uninterrupted daily rest.

Conditions to be met include:

- decrease in economic turnover: (i) not less than 15%, calculated as the relation of total turnover over two consecutive months in the period after 1 January 2020–31 December 2019, to the total turnover from the corresponding two months of the previous year following the occurrence of COVID-19 to the day preceding the day on which the employer decides to reduce uninterrupted rest or to take action to conclude an agreement on less favourable conditions of employment; or (ii) not less than 25%, calculated as the relation of total turnover during any freely indicated month in the period after 1 January 2020to the day preceding the day on which the employer decides to reduce uninterrupted rest or to take action to conclude an agreement on less favourable conditions of employment, compared to the turnover of the previous month; or (iii) an increase in the quotient of the cost of remuneration of employees, including social security contributions of employees financed by the employer, and the revenue from the sale of goods or services from the same calendar month chosen by the entrepreneur from 1 March 2020 to the day preceding the day on which the employer decides to reduce uninterrupted rest or to take action to conclude an agreement on less favourable conditions of employment, by not less than 5% in comparison with such quotient of the turnover of the preceding month;

- no tax arrears on account of contributions for social security, health insurance, the Labour Fund or the Fund by the end of the third quarter of 2019.

The employer's decision to reduce the daily and weekly rest, based on new COVID-19 regulations, is discretionary and does not require any consultations, arrangements or collective agreements.

Legal solutions for foreigners

For the duration of the pandemic, there have been implemented special solutions regarding foreigners, providing, *inter alia*, an extension until the thirtieth day following the recall of the state of epidemic/state of epidemic emergency of:

- legal stay of foreigners on the basis of national visas and temporary residence permits;
- the deadline for submitting applications for legalization of stay;
- validity of work permits, seasonal work permits and declarations on entrusting work to a foreigner, the validity of which would expire during an epidemic threat/epidemic;
- extension of legal stay for foreigners staying in Poland on the basis of visa-free travel, uniform Schengen visas and residence permits issued by other countries of the Schengen area, extend the validity of residence cards and temporary identity certificates of a foreigner and extending the validity of Pole's Cards up to three months from the date of cancellation of the state of epidemic threat/epidemic.

Thus, the residence permits and permits listed above remain valid due to the ongoing epidemic in Poland.

Legal Compliance in Poland

1. LEGAL FRAMEWORK: EMPLOYMENT LAWS

The following is the outline of sources of Polish employment laws.

The Constitution introduces some basic and fundamental rights for all employees in Poland, which are developed in more specific legal acts, e.g., the freedom of choosing and performing a particular profession or the right for participating in the social security system.

The European Employment Law includes *the Treaties* (Rome, Maastricht, Amsterdam, Nice and Lisbon Treaties); *Regulations* (e.g., the Work and Safety at Work Regulations); *Directives* (e.g., the Equal Pay Directive and the Equal Treatment Directive). The European Employment Law continues to have a major impact on national employment law in the areas of sex discrimination, equal pay, the transfer of undertakings and health and safety regulations.

The International Employment Law should be mentioned as well. Poland is a party to different international organizations passing their own legal instruments, e.g., the United Nations and its specialized body – International Labour Organization.

The national statutes with a leading position of the *Labour Code include rights and obligations of employers and employees.* Its scope includes particularly individual labour contracts and collective labour agreements. In situations referring to the employment contract but not regulated by the Labour Code, the rules of the *Civil Code* can be applied subsidiary. Moreover, some regulations of a general character are specified in other subsidiary statutes. These are called *codes of practice* and are addressed to the performers of specific professions, e.g., teachers, public prosecutors or military servants. Another set of national acts regulates *collective labour law*, e.g., Trade Unions Act, Employers' Organization Act or Resolving Collective Disputes Act.

Moving on, the *collective labour agreements* concluded between a particular employer and a trade union operating within his/her undertaking are to be presented. These acts are setting the employees' rights regarding the compensation and social benefits and subsequently should be implied in every single employment contract within a particular undertaking. Additionally, other forms of collective agreements are permitted, referring to, e.g., layoffs, resolving collective disputes.

2. CONTRACTS OF EMPLOYMENT

2.1. Overview

A contract of employment is the basic form under which work is performed. An employee undertakes to provide work of a given kind personally for, and under the supervision of, an employer and in a place and at a time specified by the employer, whereas the employer commits himself/herself to employ the employee against remuneration. Parties to the contract of employment do not enjoy full freedom in shaping the content of the contract of employment as they are subject to some statutory limitations stated in the Labour Code and other provisions, which are generally in the interest and to the advantage of the employee.

2.2. Written Employment Contracts

According to the Labour Code, each contract of employment should be made in writing. The contract should indicate parties, type of contract, its conclusion date as well as pay and working conditions, and in particular kind of work, place of work, remuneration for work broken down into its components, working time and work commencement date. If the contract of employment does not state the work commencement date, the date of the contract is assumed as the work commencement date.

If the contract is not made in writing, the employer should, before the date on which the employee commenced work at the latest, confirm the conditions of the contract in writing, in particular arrangements regarding parties, kind of contract and its conditions.

Moreover, within seven days of the contract conclusion, the employer is obliged to notify the employee in writing of daily and weekly working time, frequency of remuneration payment, holiday entitlement, applicable termination period and collective bargaining agreement by which the employee is covered.

However, if no work regulations by laws apply at the workplace (this refers only to employers employing no more than fifty employees), the employer also informs its employees about night time, place and time of remuneration payment and manner of confirming by employees their entrance time and attendance at work as well as giving reasons for their absence from work.

Any amendments to the contract of employment and conditions specified in the information provided to employees also need to be made in writing.

Failure to provide a written form of a contract of employment or its amendments does not result in its invalidity since the contract of employment becomes effective when the employee is allowed to work.

2.3. Oral Contracts

Under the Labour Code, each contract of employment should be made in writing, irrespective of its kind. However, a failure to provide a written form does not render such contract invalid but may result in a fine for an employer or in evidentiary problems in court proceedings, if any. Currently, if an employment contract is not made in written form, the employer is obliged to confirm the rules of employment to the employee before the date on which the employee commenced work of the latest.

2.4. Employee Handbooks

Polish law does not oblige employers to run employee handbooks. However, many employers introduce general rules of conduct applicable to the company. When drafting such rules, employers should pay special attention so that individual provisions do not infringe on employees' anti-discrimination rules as well as their privacy rights.

2.5. Job Descriptions

The type of agreed work is an essential and indispensable part of each contract of employment. This may be specified in general by indicating a name of a post or in detail by determining individual acts, scope of duties and responsibility. In the former case, the employer could freely instruct employees to provide certain work, whereas when the scope of duties is precisely determined, any change would require changes to the contract of employment.

Pursuant to the Labour Code, the employer may entrust the employee with a different scope of duties than the one determined in the contract of employment only for a period not exceeding three months in a calendar year. This may not result in a reduction in remuneration, and new duties should correspond to the employee's qualifications.

The scope of duties may be determined at the time of concluding a contract of employment or at a later date. However, the employer is under no obligation to provide the scope of the employee's duties in writing. The employee may be informed about the scope of his/her duties also orally. A written form is recommended for evidentiary purpose in case of a potential dispute over the scope of duties covered by the contract of employment.

2.6. Offer Letters

The Labour Code does not regulate offer letters. However, they may be concluded on the basis of Article 300 of the Labour Code in conjunction with Article 389 of the Civil Code. Such an offer letter should specify the essential terms and conditions of the promised contract and its conclusion date. No special form is required; however, a written form is recommended for evidentiary purposes.

If one of the parties (future employer or employee) evades concluding a contract of employment, the other party may seek compensation for damage suffered as a result of relying on concluding a promised contract. The compensation amount is not specified; however, in practice, it does not exceed three months' remuneration determined in the offer letter.

Moreover, instead of compensation, an employee may demand in court that a contract of employment should be concluded.

However, an employer may only claim compensation from the employee, as the latter may not be forced in court to enter into the contract of employment.

2.7. Checklist of Dos and Do Nots

- Confirm a contract of employment in writing.
- Inform an employee about employment conditions in writing within seven days from the date of conclusion of the employment agreement.
- Inform an employee about his/her scope of duties prior to work commencement.

3. RECRUITING, INTERVIEWING, SCREENING AND HIRING EMPLOYEES

3.1. Overview

Polish laws do not impose on employers any special obligations in terms of the recruitment process. Employers apply different methods of recruiting employees.

3.2. Recruiting

Recruitment of employees may be both internal and external. Internal recruitment means filling a new post with a person already employed. Employers very often choose that option as provisions of the Labour Code impose on the employer an obligation to inform all the employed about a possibility of full or part-time employment and to inform those employed for a definite period of time about vacancies.

Such information is provided in a manner customary to a given workplace, e.g., by announcing on the information board or the intranet.

The second frequently applied method is external recruitment. Employers use one of the below:

- services of a recruitment agency;
- services of an employment agency;
- publishing an announcement in the media (press, Internet);
- services of an employment office;
- participating in an employment fair for graduates;
- organizing internships for students and graduates.

When preparing job offers, employers must remember not to specify their requirements as to gender, age, denomination, etc., as this is tantamount to discrimination against candidates for employees.

3.3. Employment Applications

Polish labour law does not require using special recruitment forms. However, employers who prefer ready forms may use recruitment forms prepared by them or published by the Minister for Family, Labour and Social Policy. No photo should be attached to a questionnaire as the legislator has found that a candidate's image may result in a refusal to employ a given person. Some employers create questionnaires for job candidates themselves and place them on their website if the recruitment is online.

3.4. Pre-employment Enquiries

The Labour Code differentiates information which may be demanded from a job candidate from information which may be obtained from an employee. A job candidate may be asked to provide the following data: first and last name, date of birth, contact details given by such person, education, qualifications and employment if required for a given post. Other personal details such as place of residence, first and last names and dates of birth of employee's children may be requested from an employee if such data is necessary for the employee to enjoy special benefits provided for by labour law. Any other information may be requested by the employer if this is essential in view of the post or if this results from special provisions, e.g., information on criminal record.

It should be emphasized that if the employer requests personal data beyond the scope specified in the provisions of labour law, the employee may refuse or provide false data. Providing false information, e.g., in connection with an employee's pregnancy, will not be tantamount to disloyalty towards a future employer and may not constitute grounds for refusal to employ.

3.5. Pre-employment Tests and Examinations

Polish law does not regulate the possibility of conducting pre-employment psychological tests on job candidates, as this issue still remains controversial.

The Labour Code enables employers to demand certain personal data when a duty to disclose it results from other provisions. Such personal data includes all kinds of psychological tests. As a result, such tests are obligatory for candidates for jobs in police, prison, Border Guards, State Protection Service, as well as for applicants for a detective's licence, as special rules explicitly impose such an obligation.

There is no legal ground for candidates for other posts to be subjected to psychological or other tests. However, psychological tests are often used when recruiting employees, especially in large companies from trade, financial and advertising sectors. Some law practitioners share the opinion that an employee's consent is sufficient to conduct psychological tests. However, according to the Act on psychological profession and psychologists' self-governing council, prior to such tests a psychologist must inform a job candidate about the purpose of the test, its course, results and the manner of sharing them. After receiving such information, a candidate for an employee may give his/her consent to such tests.

Psychological tests may be applied to candidates selected by employment agencies. Pursuant to the Act on promotion of employment and institutions of labour market, an employment agency may provide so-called career counselling by which an agency helps employers select candidates for posts requiring special psychophysical aptitude.

That is why, due to existing controversies over the admissibility of psychological tests, employers often hire employment agencies to recruit staff.

It is only admissible to subject a candidate to some knowledge tests in order to check his/her skills required for a given post.

Moreover, employees are subject to mandatory pre-employment medical examinations. Their aim is to determine whether given work which the employee is to perform will not threaten his/her health. Therefore, medical examinations are obligatory for all new employees. If a candidate refuses to undergo such preliminary medical examinations, an employer has no right to employ him/her since a medical certificate is indispensable to allow an employee to work.

Employers should ensure the protection of materials obtained from candidates during the recruitment process. According to the decisions of the President of the Personal Data Protection Office (PPDPO), an employer as data administrator is obliged to ensure safety of data and, if such data is not indispensable for the purpose for which it was gathered, he/she should order their removal.

3.6. Background, Reference and Credit Checks

Checking references and collecting opinion on the job candidate from former employers or persons with whom he/she cooperated is an effective way of verifying data presented by an employee. Polish provisions do not provide for an obligation to issue references; however, an employer may, at the request of its former employee, issue a document evaluating employee's work.

Polish law excludes credit checks of employees unless this is required by relevant provisions of law due to the specificity of the post. Also, gathering background information about the job candidate by detectives or so-called information agencies is against the law.

3.7. Interviewing

A job interview is the most important element of the recruitment process. Its purpose is to collect information on skills, knowledge and professional experience of the candidate which is required for a given job. Therefore, an employer may ask the candidate about his/her education, universities/ colleges he/she graduated from, all specialist and language courses he/she attended to as well as about previous workplaces, positions held and experience gained but only if required for a given job.

An employer may not ask about personal life, marital status, family or personal plans of the candidate for an employee.

Moreover, an employer must make sure that he/she does not ask questions breaching equal treatment and anti-discrimination rules. An example of such a discriminatory question would be to ask about planned pregnancy. Such a question will not be tantamount to a breach of an equal treatment rule if this information is required for a given post, conditions of the post or professional requirements for employees, e.g., when a woman applies for a job listed as a job prohibited for pregnant women.

3.8. Hiring Procedures

After deciding to hire a job candidate, an employer is obliged to:

- direct an employee to mandatory medical examinations prior to allowing him/her to work;
- inform an employee about occupational health and safety (OHS) procedures applicable at the company;
- enter into a contract of employment or confirm contract terms and conditions in writing;
- inform an employee about working conditions within seven days from the date of conclusion of the employment agreement;
- inform an employee about internal labour law regulations, such as pay and working conditions;
- register an employee with the Social Insurance Authority within seven days of work commencement.

3.9. Fines and Penalties

If an equal treatment rule is infringed when entering into an employment relationship, a job candidate may seek in court damages of at least PLN 3,010 (ca. EUR 670). In practice, courts award much higher amounts if a candidate shows a connection between an employer taking into account discriminatory features and a refusal to enter into an employment relationship, as well as how this led to damage suffered by a candidate, e.g., loss of profits during a certain term of contract. In practice, courts generally assume a three-month period as this is the maximum term of a contract of employment for a trial period.

3.10. Checklist of Dos and Do Nots

- Do not request other personal data than specified in the Labour Code, unless allowed by special provisions.
- Avoid discriminatory terms such as gender or age in job advertisements.
- Direct an employee to pre-employment medical examination prior to allowing him/her to work.
- Ensure an OHS training to an employee prior to work commencement.
- Inform an employee about internal labour law regulations such as work regulations, remuneration rules, equal treatment rules.

4. MANAGING PERFORMANCE/CONDUCT

4.1. Overview

Polish labour law does not provide regulations determining the manner of evaluation and professional development of an employee. As a result, employers are not obliged to introduce internal rules for periodical evaluations of employees. However, many employers introduce such internal regulations/questionnaires of evaluation aimed at verifying employee's achievements and periodically conduct evaluating talks with employees. Such documents may be used as evidence before a labour court in case when an employer terminates a contract of employment because of a low efficiency of an employee.

4.2. Coaching and Counselling

Not applicable.

4.3. Written Evaluations

Although Polish provisions of labour law do not impose on employers an obligation to evaluate employees, many employers, in order to verify professional achievements of employees, apply an evaluation system uniform for all employees. Such a system often constitutes a basis for awarding higher remuneration or discretionary bonus to an employee. It is based on a questionnaire used to evaluate an employee in writing. A questionnaire is signed both by an employer and an employee. When evaluating an employee, an employer must ensure objectivity so that evaluation is not based on discriminatory features but takes into account mainly employee's knowledge, skills and engagement, as well as his/her attitude towards co-workers and clients and care for the welfare of the company.

4.4. Warning and Suspensions

The penalties are provided for in Polish labour law as a measure of enforcing compliance with basic employees' obligations generally related to work order and to penalize the violations, without dismissing employees. It is not necessary to first penalize the employee for his/her actions in order to be able to terminate employment. According to the jurisprudence of the Polish Supreme Court, nothing prevents terminating the employment on the basis of the same event for which the employee was charged with a penalty when the seriousness of this misconduct is so significant that the circumstances and consequences (even potential) of its committing justify the employer's belief that it is impossible to continue hiring the employee.

Employers are entitled to impose the following penalties on employees for non-compliance with the work order: warning, reprimand and pecuniary penalty. Warning or reprimand can be imposed in cases of less significant violations, such as late arrivals at work, improper way of justifying absence from work, non-compliance with work regulations, minor violations related to OHS rules.

According to the jurisprudence of the Polish Supreme Court, warning is the least severe penalty and can be imposed even if an employee's fault is minor. Reprimand is more severe and qualifies for situations where the employee's fault is of a higher degree. The pecuniary penalty can be imposed only in cases of more serious violations of OHS rules and fire protection provisions, leaving work or absence from work without excuse, drinking alcohol at work and coming to work intoxicated.

The single pecuniary penalty can amount up to a daily remuneration rate of the employee, and their sum cannot exceed one-tenth of monthly remuneration payable to the employee after deductions permitted under the law (if any). In any case, the pecuniary penalties cannot reduce the monthly salary below the amount of approximately PLN 2,709 (ca. EUR 600) (i.e., 90% of the minimum statutory remuneration in 2021). The penalty should be imposed within two weeks from the date on which the employer became aware of the violation, but not later than three months from the date of violation.

An employer needs to hear out an employee in order to give him/her a chance to explain his/her actions before the penalty is imposed. In practice, the employer can take a record of the hearing. After the hearing, the penalty may be imposed and the employer needs to notify the employee in writing of the type of penalty, type and date of committed violation, right to file an objection with the employer within seven days.

If the objection was filed, the employer needs to request an opinion of a trade union representing the employee (if any) in this respect and has fourteen days to reject or accept the objection. If, within the fourteen-day period, the employer does not expressly reject the objection, it is deemed that it was accepted by the employer and the penalty is nullified. If the objection was rejected, the employee could file a statement of claims to a labour court for revoking the penalty, within fourteen days from receiving a rejection notice.

Information on imposed penalty needs to be kept in personal files for a period of one year (if no new penalties were imposed on an employee). It can be removed sooner if, e.g., the labour court revokes the penalty.

4.5. Checklist of Dos and Do Nots

- Hear out the employee before imposing the penalty.
- Request opinion of the trade unions if the employee files an objection.
- Remove the information about the penalty from personal files after one year if there were no further violations during that period.

5. TERMINATION OF EMPLOYEES FOR PERFORMANCE OR DISCIPLINARY REASONS

5.1. Overview

Under Polish law, an employer may terminate a contract of employment for an employee's fault by submitting:

- a letter of termination with notice period;
- a letter of termination without notice period.

A letter of termination with notice period as well as a letter of termination without notice period should be made in writing and effectively submitted, which means that an employee should be able to read it. It does not matter, though, whether an employee has really read it but that he/she has such a possibility. In practice, it is recommended to ask the employee to sign such termination letter to confirm that he/she has received it.

When terminating an indefinite term employment contract with or without notice period, an employer has to provide reasons for termination. Failure to give reasons or providing too general or false reasons may give rise to an employee's claim for finding termination ineffective, for reinstatement or for damages.

Each termination letter should contain information about the employee's right to appeal against termination to the labour court. Failure to provide such information results in restoring a time limit for appeal by the employee to the labour court.

5.2. Termination upon Notice

5.2.1. Indefinite Term Employment Contract

When terminating an employment contract an employer must observe a proper notice period. A notice period depends on the length of employment with a given employer and amounts to:

- two weeks if an employee has been employed for less than six months;
- one month if an employee has been employed for at least six months;
- three months if an employee has been employed for at least three years.

With regard to employees who are financially responsible for property entrusted to them as part of their duties, a two-week notice period may be extended in the employment contract up to one month, and a one-month notice period up to three months.

Termination of an employment contract is always effective at the end of the month (if termination counts in months) or at the end of the week on Saturday (if termination counts in weeks).

Special protection against termination covers:

- Employees who have no more than four years left to attain the retirement age and who upon attaining that age will be entitled to pension.
- Employees on leave or absent from work for a justified reason.
- Pregnant women.
- Employees who applied for childcare leave – a contract of employment may not be terminated in a period from the day of applying for such leave to the date when such leave ends.
- Employees entitled to childcare leave who applied for having their working time reduced – a contract of employment may not be terminated in a period from the day of applying for reduction to the date when the previous working time starts to apply. The period of reduction may not exceed twelve months.

– Trade union activists.

An employer who intends to terminate an employment contract upon notice with an employee with whom an indefinite term employment contract has been concluded should provide the trade union which represents the employee with written information of its intention and state reasons for termination. The trade union may raise objections to termination within five days of notification. The employer may not terminate employment without taking the aforesaid objections into consideration. If the trade union provides its objections within five days or does not provide it at all, the employer may terminate employment, while taking the statement of the trade union into consideration. According to the newest jurisprudence of the Polish Supreme Court, the significance of conducting consultation in a written form cannot be reduced to the mere proof of the act of consulting the intention to terminate employment. The required written form opens the consultation procedure provided for in the Labour Code, i.e., a specific sequence of actions (events and behaviours) and deadlines required from the employer and the trade union. The reservation of the written form is not adopted only for evidential purposes but constitutes an unambiguous legal norm, the violation of which is subject to a sanction and thus, should not be neglected by the employers.

5.2.2. Contract for a Trial Period

A contract for a trial period may be concluded with a given employee for a maximum period of three months. The purpose of concluding such a contract is to verify the professional skills of an employee. Such agreement may precede any of the types of employment contracts described in this section. The employer is not obliged to continue the employment relationship after a lapse of a trial period. Such a contract may be terminated by either party by notice. A notice period equals:

– three working days if the trial period does not exceed two weeks;
– one week if the trial period exceeds two weeks;
– two weeks if the trial period is three months.

Special protection against termination covers pregnant women for whom a contract for a trial period exceeding one month is extended to the day of childbirth if such contract would normally terminate after the third month of pregnancy.

When terminating a contract for a trial period, there is no need to state the reasons for termination.

A contract for a trial period may be concluded several times between the same parties, if:

- the employee is to be employed to perform a different type of work, or
- after three years from the termination of the employment relationship (termination or expiry of the employment contract), the employee is to be employed for the purpose of performing work of the same type.

The provision does not limit the number of contracts for a trial period that may be concluded between the parties in case the employee is to be employed to perform a different type of work. However, it is essential that the employee is hired 'for a different type of work'. This should be understood as work that is generically different, i.e., work in a different position and with a different scope of duties than before. It is not enough to name differently a job position where the employee is to be re-employed. It is important to define differently the scope of duties performed under a new contract for a trial period than performed under the previous contract. It is the job descriptions, and not only the job title that should also be used to determine whether we are dealing with a 'different type of job' that allows the conclusion of another employment contract for a trial period.

5.2.3. Definite Term Employment Contract

A definite term employment contract, as well as an indefinite term employment contract, may be terminated with a proper notice period.

Special protection against termination covers pregnant women for whom a contract for a definite period is extended up to the day of childbirth if the contract would normally terminate after the third month of pregnancy.

The notice period for fixed-term contracts depends on the length of service with the current employer and amounts to:

- two weeks if an employee has been employed less than six months;
- one month if an employee has been employed for at least six months;
- three months if an employee has been employed for at least three years.

5.2.4. Replacement Contract

Replacement contracts are no longer in use. If the employer will replace another employee, there is a possibility to conclude a contract for a definite period of time. A notice period of a contract concluded for a definite period of time depends on the length of service with the current employer. The respective notice periods are as follows:

- two weeks if an employee has been employed less than six months;
- one month if an employee has been employed for at least six months;
- three months if an employee has been employed for at least three years.

For such contracts, no provisions on special protection of pregnant women apply, which means that a replacement contract is not extended to the date of childbirth if the contract would normally terminate after the third month of pregnancy.

5.2.5. Termination of the Employment Contract Without Notice Period

Termination by the employer of the employment contract without notice period means that employment ceases upon submitting a termination letter to an employee. Every employment contract may be terminated this way, provided that the following conditions are jointly met:

(a) Occurrence of one of the reasons enabling termination of the employment contract, for example:
   (i) Glaring breach by an employee of his/her duties;
   (ii) Crime committed by an employee, preventing further employment at a given post if the crime is evident or has been ascertained by a final judgment;
   (iii) Loss of employee's qualifications necessary to perform work at a given post, through employee's fault.
(b) Submitting a termination letter within one month from the day when the employer learnt about the reason referred to above.
(c) Requesting an opinion (in some cases, consent) from the trade union, which represents an employee. The employer should consult its intention to terminate an employment contract without notice with the trade unions active in the employment establishment. In such a case, the trade union should state its opinion within three days.
(d) Submitting a termination letter in writing with reasons for termination.

5.3. Separation/Severance Pay

Under Polish law, an employer is not obliged to pay compensation to an employee unless internal regulations require this or termination of an employment contract is not caused by an employee.

It should be noted that an employee may appeal against termination of the employment contract to the labour court. Should the labour court find the termination of the indefinite term contract unjustified or that it violates the provisions on termination of contracts, it may, upon the employee's request, declare the notice of termination ineffective. If the contract has already been terminated, the court can reinstate the employee. Should that be deemed impossible, the court may award compensation, which is the most common practice. The compensation shall amount to remuneration due for a period ranging from two weeks to three months, but not less than remuneration for the period of notice (subject to the court's decision).

Should the labour court reinstate the employee and the employee resumes employment, he/she shall have a right to remuneration for the period when he/she was unemployed but not longer than two months, and if the period of notice is three months, for no longer than one month.

However, it may not be excluded that, based on the latest judicial decisions, when an employer unlawfully terminates a contract of employment without notice, an employee may seek under civil law higher damages than remuneration for the notice period.

Should the employment contract be terminated with an employee who has not less than four years left until he/she reaches retirement age (if the period of employment allows him/her to acquire the right to a retirement pension), with a pregnant employee or an employee on maternity/paternity leave, the remuneration shall be paid for the entire period for which the employee is unemployed.

5.4. Fines and Penalties

Employers for terminating a contract of employment with or without notice in glaring violation of Polish law may be fined up to PLN 30,000 (ca. EUR 6,670). It must be noted that such penalties are used rarely.

5.5. Checklist of Dos and Do Nots

- Terminate the contract in writing. Failure to provide a written form by an employer is a breach of law. If an employee whose contract of employment has been terminated contrary to the law refers the case to court, he/she may be reinstated under the previous conditions or compensated. If the employee does not wish to raise a claim, such termination of the contract of employment will be effective despite infringing the law.

- Ask the employee to acknowledge receipt with his/her signature or send it via registered mail.
- State reasons for termination of an indefinite term contract of employment with or without notice as well as for termination of a definite term employment contract without notice.
- Check if the employee enjoys special rights of protection against termination of a contract of employment.

6. LAYOFFS, REDUCTIONS IN FORCE AND/OR REDUNDANCIES AS A RESULT OF JOB ELIMINATIONS OR OTHER RESTRUCTURING

6.1. Overview

An employer who wishes to dismiss employees due to job elimination or restructuring should apply a common procedure provided for in the Labour Code or special procedure regulated in the Act on special principles of terminating employment due to reasons not attributable to employees, also known as the Layoff Act. The number of employees is essential when deciding which procedure to follow. If the employer employs at least twenty persons, it should apply a special procedure specified in the Layoff Act.

'Reasons not attributable to employees' are not defined. In practice, they cover economic reasons regarding only an employer, mainly restructuring, elimination of jobs and change of the employer's activity profile.

However, if job elimination is stated as a reason for termination, this must be real and exist at the time of termination, which means in practice that there are no doubts that the job will be eliminated. Although courts do not verify the legitimacy of restructuring and the employer's decision about the usefulness of maintaining a given job, they may hold that job elimination was only apparent. And this may give rise to a claim for reinstatement or damages. Organizational changes aimed at reducing employment must be real. Based on judicial decisions, apparent job elimination occurs when the job is eliminated but another job is created instead (with a different name) which does not differ significantly from the one which has been eliminated.

For mass layoffs, it is required to meet certain conditions regarding a period during which layoffs are to be made, as well as the number of people covered by the layoff. According to the statutory definition, the mass layoff exists when, within thirty days, it covers at least:

- ten employees, when the employer employs fewer than 100 people.
- ten per cent of employees, when the employer employs from 100 to 299 people.
- thirty employees, when the employer employs at least 300 people.

The Layoff Act facilitates employers to conduct layoffs due to economic reasons, and at the same time protects employees by ensuring them a severance pay. Moreover, the statute introduces a special consultation and information procedure for trade unions (and if there are no trade unions at the company – for representatives of employees) and for a relevant district employment office.

6.2. Reductions in Force/Layoffs/Job Eliminations

The labour court does not verify the legitimacy of the employer's decision on changing the organizational structure of the workplace in order to rationalize and limit the number of employees. However, the court assesses whether the employer applied justified criteria for selecting employees for jobs and for choosing employees to be dismissed.

When applying a layoff procedure, the employer is obliged to:

(i) consult the company's trade union;
(ii) inform the employment office; and
(iii) consult the company's works council.

6.2.1 Consultation with the Trade Union

An employer intending to lay off employees due to reasons attributable to the employer is obliged to consult trade unions about layoffs (if there are no such trade unions, the employer consults representatives of its employees). Such consultations should cover among other things:

- possibility of avoiding layoff;
- possibility of reducing the extent of layoff;
- employment matters connected with the planned layoff (e.g., a possibility of retraining and obtaining another job by employees to be laid off).

Within a period not longer than twenty days from the date of such notification, the employer and the trade union shall negotiate and conclude a layoff agreement.

The layoff agreement shall specify the rules of procedure in matters regarding employees covered by the intended layoff and the employer's obligations necessary to solve other employment-related issues connected with the planned layoff. The agreement shall cover in particular:

- dates of making employees redundant;
- layoff criteria;
- holiday entitlement or payment of an equivalent for unused holiday;

– increase in severance pay beyond the threshold specified in the statute;
– outplacement activities.

If the employer and the trade union are not able to agree on the terms of such layoff agreement, the employer may determine, via internal regulations, the manner of executing layoff in its sole discretion.

6.2.2. Information to the Employment Office

Before starting the layoff procedure (the exact date is not specified by law), the employer shall provide the competent district employment office with such written information regarding the layoff as has been submitted also to the trade union (first notification).

The employer shall further notify (second notification) the competent district employment office in writing of adopted settlements in regard to the layoff, including information on the number of employees to be laid off, as well as reasons for the layoff, period within which the layoff is to take place and the consultation conducted with the trade union. The second notification shall be made after the conclusion of the layoff agreement with the trade union, and if no layoff agreement was concluded, after having prepared the respective internal regulations.

6.2.3. Consultation with the Works Councils

The employer shall also provide the company's works council with information on:

– activity and economic situation of the employer and expected changes;
– status, structure and expected changes to employment, as well as activities aimed at maintaining the employment level;
– activities which may cause essential changes to the organization of work and employment bases.

The employer should also hold consultations with the works council in this respect. The employer is not bound by the result of the consultations and opinion of the works council. Consultations with the works council should be held irrespective of negotiations with the trade unions, as discussed above.

There is no specific statutory period for providing information to the works council and for holding consultations. However, information should be provided timely to enable the works council to get familiar with the information and prepare its standing.

6.2.4. Protected Employees

The Layoff Act modifies regulations concerning employees specially protected against termination. During a period of special protection, the employer may only change current pay and working conditions, which means that the employer offers the employee new payment regulations (e.g., lower salary) or new working conditions (e.g., different tasks or different working time). If the employee accepts such new conditions, they will start to apply after the lapse of the notice period. If the employee does not agree to the new conditions, termination of the employment contract will become effective after the lapse of the notice period.

If the change of pay and working conditions results in the reduction of remuneration, the above-mentioned employees are entitled to receive compensatory allowance until the end of the period in which they would be specially protected against termination.

The above limitations in terms of terminating contracts of employment with protected employees are not applicable in the event of winding up the company. Under the Layoff Act, the employer may provide the employee with a termination letter only after notifying a district employment office, and termination of employment may be effective after thirty days of such notification.

6.2.5. Severance Pay

As a result of applying a layoff procedure, an employee is entitled to a severance pay in the amount depending on the length of employment with a given employer:

- severance pay equal to one month's remuneration if an employee has been employed with a given employer fewer than two years;
- severance pay equal to two month's remuneration if an employee has been employed with a given employer from two to eight years;
- severance pay equal to three months' remuneration if an employee has been employed with a given employer for more than eight years.

The amount of severance pay is calculated in the same manner as a cash equivalent for holiday. Severance pay may not exceed fifteen times the minimum remuneration for work, namely PLN 45,150.00 (ca. EUR 9,104) in 2022.

The statute protects employees by ensuring them a possibility of being re-employed with the same employer if the employer employs again employees from the same profession, and the employee informs about his/her intention to resume employment.

6.2.6. Outplacement

Furthermore, an employer wishing to lay off at least fifty employees within three months is obliged to take some outplacement activities, which means that the employer should consult a relevant local employment office competent for the seat of the employer or for the place where work is performed about a scope and form of assistance for employees being laid off, in particular about:

- job placement;
- professional consulting;
- training;
- assistance in active job searching.

6.2.7. Criteria for the Selection of Employees

Polish law does not provide for a detailed list of legally justified criteria which should be taken into account when selecting employees to be laid off. In particular, there is no legal definition of 'social criteria'. However, the decisions of the Supreme Court, as well as the doctrine of labour law, have developed guidelines according to which adequate criteria should be based on the objective and just evaluation of employees and the results of their work. The assessment of legitimacy of layoffs should take into account a legally justified interest of an employer and features of an employee with respect to his/her employment. The employer may consider the employee's usefulness for the employment establishment or the fact as to whether the employee ensures proper functioning of the employment establishment. The criteria determined by the Supreme Court and the doctrine include professional skills and experience, course of employment, availability of an employee during standard working hours, involvement in work, manner of fulfilling obligations, length of service. It is advisable that the employer selects employees on the basis of at least two criteria. According to the jurisprudence of the Supreme Court criteria for selection of the employee for dismissal, as a supplement to the generally specified reason for termination of the employment relationship (most often indicated as organizational changes), shows the entire context in which the dismissal of a particular person took place and allows the employee to understand why it was him/her who was made the statement of intent of that kind. It also allows attempting to undermine the legitimacy of the employer's termination of employment. Social criteria which the employer may take into account include: personal, family and financial situation of an employee, that is: (i) whether an employee is the only working member in the family, (ii) difficult personal situation, (iii) health of an employee and/or members of his/her family, (iv) additional source of income, (v) possibilities on the labour market.

Social criteria are of a supplementary nature, which means that they should be considered if general criteria are not sufficient to select employees to be laid off. For instance, if it is necessary to lay off one of two or more employees with the same skills and qualifications and the same length of service, the employer may also take social criteria into account.

It should be emphasized that any discriminative criteria, such as age or gender, are inadmissible.

However, according to the Polish Supreme Court decision of 20 May 2020 (case file no. I PK 110/19) reaching the retirement age is a socially justifiable criterion for selecting employees for dismissal, thus cannot be regarded as discriminatory against a specific group of employees whose employment relationships are terminated by their employer. Consequently, such a criterion for selection for dismissal does not constitute discrimination or unequal treatment of the employee in comparison with employees who could not yet enjoy pension rights in the event of potential loss of employment.

6.2.8. Individual Redundancy

The Layoff Act may also be applicable to dismissals of a fewer number of employees than the above-mentioned (individual dismissal), provided that the employer employs at least twenty people and the only reasons for termination are those not attributable to employees. In the case of individual dismissals, the above-mentioned consultation and information procedure does not apply.

6.3. Fines and Penalties

Both missing the deadlines for providing notification to the district employment office and failure to notify an employees' representative (trade unions and works council) and to issue a layoff agreement infringe the provisions on terminating contracts of employment and result in certain consequences for the employer. If the court finds that termination of an indefinite term contract of employment is unjustified or infringes the provisions on terminating contracts of employment, a labour court, at the employee's request, adjudges that the termination is ineffective and, if the contract has already been terminated, it may adjudge that the employee be reinstated under the previous terms and conditions or be compensated. The labour court may not consider the employee's request to find termination or request for reinstatement ineffective if it has established that considering such a request would be impossible or pointless. Then, the court awards compensation. The compensation is equal to remuneration for a period from two weeks to three months, but not lower than remuneration for the termination period.

6.4. Checklist of Dos and Do Nots

- Ensure that reorganization of employment, including job elimination, is not apparent.
- Inform trade unions and representatives of employees (if there are no trade unions) about planned layoffs.
- Enter into an agreement with trade unions or issue regulations to agree on a plan for group dismissal and indicate criteria for layoffs.
- Notify the district employment office of planned layoffs and arrangements with trade unions.
- Check if employees to be dismissed enjoy special rights of protection against termination of a contract of employment.

7. LABOUR AND EMPLOYMENT LAW RAMIFICATIONS UPON ACQUISITION OR SALE OF A BUSINESS

7.1. Overview

Poland has implemented EC Directive 2001/23/EC of 12 March 2001 on the approximation of the laws of the Member States relating to the safeguarding of employees rights in the event of transfers of undertakings, businesses or parts of undertakings or businesses. Polish law does not define the transfer of a business or acts of law resulting in such transfer. Judicial decisions state that a business (workplace) is transferred to a new employer when a given act of law or event causes assets or employment-related tasks or functions to transfer from one entity (current employer) to another (new employer). In consequence, the current employer does not need such employees to work for it anymore. Employees pass on from the seller to the purchaser. In practice, the transfer may be based on a business (organized part of business) sale agreement, lease agreement, merger or outsourcing.

The transfer is effected *ex lege*, namely, a seller and purchaser do not need to perform any special acts of law for employees to be transferred. The transfer of a business may not be avoided, for instance, by not informing employees as required. It covers all employees of the business or its part intended to be transferred, no matter whether they object or not. It is impossible to choose only some employees to be transferred.

Based on judicial decisions, in case of doubt, the date of transfer is when the property (such as business) is acquired and not when, for example, a sale agreement is signed.

The transfer results in a change of an employer and assuming rights and obligations of the current employer (e.g., seller) by a new employer (e.g., purchaser) with regard to employment relationships existing at the time of transfer (also those during notice period but not those finally terminated prior to the transfer date). Employment contracts are still binding, and the period of termination is not interrupted.

In principle, provisions of the collective bargaining agreement, if any, which relate to employees to be transferred, are still in force (for one year).

7.2. Acquisition of a Business

The transfer of a business causes the acquisition of all rights and obligations resulting from the employment relationships with the seller. Therefore, prior to transfer, purchasers become familiar with a legal and employment situation of the business being taken over, in particular with any claims of employees and obligations of the seller.

At least thirty days prior to the planned transfer date, a purchaser has to inform its employees in writing about: the planned transfer date, reasons for transfer and legal, economic and social consequences for employees, as well as planned changes or other actions regarding employment conditions and retraining (e.g., changes to working or pay regulations, change of place of work).

In practice, such information is often provided to employees being taken over.

The purchaser submits the above information on the transfer to trade unions in the above period. Generally, employers often pass information on about the transfer both to trade unions and individually to employees (despite the fact that provisions oblige them only to notify trade unions active at the workplace).

The purchaser negotiates with its trade unions, for a period of thirty days (starting on the date of providing information on the transfer) on planned changes to employment as a result of the transfer (e.g., changes of workplace, work organization, pay or working rules).

If no agreement is reached, a purchaser may individually determine such changes, taking into account arrangements made during negotiations.

A purchaser should provide its works council (if created) with information on:

- planned transfer;
- planned changes to employment conditions; and
- carrying out non-binding negotiations in this regard (regardless of informing employees or trade unions).

There is no specific time to provide such information; however, it should be long enough so as to enable the works council to become familiar with it, present their standpoint and prepare for consultations. In practice, information is often submitted together with information for trade unions and employees.

Detailed regulations regarding information and consultation may be inserted in the agreement between the works council and the employer.

Breach of information obligation by the purchaser may not cause negative consequences for employees, e.g., impede the exercise of their rights as a result of the transfer.

A purchaser may be held liable for damage caused to employees for failing to inform them about the transfer.

Moreover, a person directly liable may be punished with:

- a fine of up to PLN 30,000 (ca. EUR 6,670) for breaching an information obligation due towards employees;
- a fine of up to PLN 5,000 (ca. EUR 1,100) or restriction of liberty for breaching obligations towards trade unions or works councils.

Within two months of the business transfer, employees who were taken over may terminate employment without notice period seven days in advance.

On the transfer date, a purchaser should offer persons employed on a different basis than the employment contract (i.e., nomination, appointment or cooperative employment contract) new pay and working conditions and set them at least a seven-day period for accepting them. Rejecting new pay and working conditions causes the current employment to terminate after the expiry of the notice period.

Persons employed under civil law agreements (contract of mandate, contract for specific work) are not covered by the transfer. A transfer of such agreements along with the business (or its part) is governed by civil law, in particular provisions on the assignment of rights.

7.2.1. Purchaser's Liability

In the event of takeover of the entire business, the purchaser is solely liable for obligations towards employees being taken over (e.g., for working overtime).

If part of the business is transferred, the purchaser and the seller are jointly and severally liable for obligations resulting from employment relationships which came into being prior to transfer (an employee may seek his/her claim in full from the seller or purchaser or from both of them at the same time, or claim to be satisfied by them in relevant parts).

A purchaser has to observe provisions of the collective bargaining agreement with respect to employees taken over (if such agreement was in force at the time of the transfer) for one year from the transfer date. Provisions of the agreement which affect the conditions of employment contracts become part of employment contracts of employees being taken over after the said one year.

If the entire business is transferred, the purchaser takes over fund means to its own fund, and if the purchaser does not keep such fund, means should be kept at a separate bank account of the purchaser.

In the event of takeover of part of business, the purchaser should receive, within thirty days of the transfer, part of means kept at the seller's fund proportionate to the number of employees being taken over. Detailed distribution rules may be specified in the agreement between a seller and purchaser.

On the transfer date, a purchaser receives from the seller personal files and employment documentation regarding employees being taken over.

Within seven days from the transfer date, a purchaser reports the takeover of employees to the Social Insurance Authority and registers itself as a payer of social insurance premiums at the same time when the seller is deregistered as a premium payer.

7.3. Acquisition Checklist

- Read employment conditions resulting from employment contracts, pay and working regulations or collective bargaining agreements and familiarize yourself with the legal situation in terms of employment relationships at a workplace.
- Inform employees and also trade unions, if any, in writing about the planned transfer at least thirty days in advance.
- Inform the works council, if any, about the planned transfer.
- If there is an employee social benefits fund at a workplace, collect means from that fund from the seller. In the event of transfer of part of business, you can determine with the seller the rules for fund means distribution in a separate agreement.
- Take personal files and employment documentation of employees being taken over from the seller.

- Report a change of the payer of social insurance premiums of employees taken over to the Social Insurance Authority within seven days of the transfer date, along with a seller's application for its deregistration.

7.4. Sale of a Business

In practice, it is recommended to indicate a group of employees covered by the transfer, by determining how their work is connected with assets or tasks being transferred.

A seller passes on to its employees (those being transferred and others) information on the transfer and its consequences in the scope and time specified in section 7.2 above.

The seller provides information to its trade unions and works council about the transfer and, if necessary, negotiates with them, according to section 7.2, on rules and extents of planned actions regarding employment conditions, e.g., change of remuneration and working conditions.

The seller is obliged to inform only trade unions about the transfer, in practice, however, employers often inform both trade unions and employees.

In addition to informing employees or trade unions, the seller should notify its works council of the planned transfer and changes to employment conditions as well as carry out non-binding consultations (*see* section 7.2 above).

Sanctions for breaching information and consultation obligations described in section 7.2 also apply to the seller.

Limitations to termination or modification of employment relationships in connection with the transfer of a business, regarding the purchaser, described in section 7.2 also apply to the seller.

The seller remains liable for obligations resulting from employment relationships and which came into being prior to the transfer date only if the purchaser acquires part of the business. In such a situation, both employers are jointly and severally liable for such obligations (*see* section 7.2 above).

The seller is also obliged to give the purchaser all or part of the means from the employee social benefits fund (*see* section 7.2 above).

Upon transfer, the seller has to provide the purchaser with personal files and employment documentation relating to employees being taken over.

Within seven days of the transfer date, the seller reports the transfer of employees to the Social Insurance Authority and deregisters itself as the payer of social insurance premiums. This act should be made at the same time as reporting the takeover of employees by the purchaser.

7.5. Sale Checklist (Current Employer)

- Inform employees and also trade unions, if any at the workplace, in writing about the planned transfer at least thirty days in advance.
- Inform the works council, if any, about the planned transfer.
- If there is an employee social benefits fund, give the purchaser means from that fund. In the event of transfer of part of business, you can determine with the purchaser the rules for fund means distribution in a separate agreement.
- Provide to the purchaser personal files and employment documentation of employees being taken over.
- Deregister yourself as a payer of premiums at the Social Insurance Authority with regard to employees taken over within seven days from the transfer date, at the same time of purchaser's registration as a premium payer.
- Keep copies of employment documentation (e.g., employment contracts concluded with employees, working rules and agreements with employees) for evidentiary purposes in case of claims of former employees.
- Do not take direct or indirect action which may worsen the purchaser's situation; e.g., do not conclude long-term agreements with employees with regard to bonuses or granting leave on favourable conditions.

8. USE OF ALTERNATIVE WORKFORCES: INDEPENDENT CONTRACTORS, CONTRACT EMPLOYEES AND TEMPORARY OR LEASED WORKERS

8.1. Overview

In Poland, an alternative form of employment includes services rendered by natural persons under civil law agreements. There is an exception to the employment of temporary workers, which is governed by labour law.

In practice, civil law based employment enables employers/principals to avoid harsh labour law regulations (in particular in terms of overtime work, mandatory severance pay, paid leave and sickness and reasons for termination) and thus reduce costs and make employment more flexible.

Alternative forms of employment may not be applied if a manner of fulfilling a given task requires subordination, namely that employees are under the direct supervision of the principal/employer as to the manner, time and place of performing work. Under the law, providing services under conditions typical for an employment relationship is treated as an employment relationship, no matter how the parties call it. Therefore, using alternative forms of employment is connected with the risk of qualifying them by the labour court (in case of a dispute with an 'employee' or at the request of the National Labour Inspectorate) as an employment relationship.

Risk of Agreement Being Qualified as Employment Contract

In order to reduce the said risk, civil law agreements in particular should not: provide for agent's subordination and provision of services under the supervision of the principal, exclude agent's liability towards third parties, limit agent's liability towards the principal or impose an obligation to perform work personally.

According to the standpoint presented in judicial decisions, if the agreement contains employment-related elements, but they do not prevail, such agreement is qualified not on the basis of its name but on the basis of the actual manner of providing services and, alternatively, whether the parties wished to conclude an employment contract or civil law agreement.

If the court adjudicates that an employment contract was in fact replaced by other forms of employment, an employer (or responsible person) may be fined up to PLN 30,000 (ca. EUR 6,670) and obliged to pay outstanding premiums for social insurance.

8.2. Independent Contractor

8.2.1. Definition

Self-employment means conducting one's own business connected with the provision of services to another entity under the civil law agreement.

This requires registration of one's business and paying social insurance premiums and taxes on remuneration individually.

As opposed to employees, the self-employed render services independently and are obliged to exercise special due diligence. They are also fully liable for damage caused in connection with the provision of services.

The self-employed keep their own accounting and make payments to the Social Insurance Authority and the Tax Office. They are also entitled to deductions from income tax and value-added tax.

8.2.2. Creating the Relationship

Cooperation with the self-employed is based on the civil law agreement (e.g., agreement for the provision of services, cooperation or mandate agreement). In practice, such an agreement should be made in writing.

A change of the form of employment from the employment contract to self-employment may create a risk that the labour court finds that such relationship is equal to employment, especially when type, manner and conditions of work are not changed.

8.2.3. Compensation

Compensation amount and payment rules should be determined in the agreement between the self-employed and the principal. As of 1 January 2017, it is obligatory to keep records of the working time of the employees employed on the basis of self-employment. Moreover, the minimum hourly rate in 2022 is in this case PLN 19.70 (ca. EUR 4.4). In practice, the self-employed often receive compensation for actually performed work (i.e., without compensation for the time of sickness) based on the monthly invoices issued by them. The principal is not obliged to incur costs of mandates and costs of conducting business by the self-employed.

8.2.4. Other Terms and Conditions

The self-employed and principals may freely agree on the provisions of the agreement in compliance with civil law. In order to avoid a risk that such an agreement may be treated as an employment contract, such agreement should not include provisions typical for employment contracts (e.g., paid leave, paid sickness leave, limited liability towards third parties).

If the agreement stipulates non-competition provisions after the expiry of cooperation, it should also provide for compensation payable to the self-employed. Such opinion is presented by the Supreme Court in one of its decisions. Compensation may be determined similarly as obligatory minimum compensation in labour law (i.e., 25% of the remuneration for a period immediately preceding termination of the employment contract equal to the length of ban on competition). It must be noted that the requirement for payment of the compensation will be assessed case by case.

8.3. Contract Workers

Employment on the basis of the civil law agreement (mandate, contract for specific work, management contract) may also apply to a natural person who does not run a sole-person business.

Individual types of civil law agreements differ among themselves. For example, under a contract of mandate a mandatory undertakes to perform certain acts for the mandator, whereas under a contract for specific work, the person undertakes to provide certain results of his/her work.

There is a risk that such agreements may be qualified as employment contracts, especially when they provide for the provision of services in a manner typical for employment relationships or when they replace employment contracts (*see* section 8.1).

Civil law agreements may be concluded in any form (contrary to employment contracts which should be concluded in writing and, if not, they should be confirmed in writing). For practical reasons, in order to avoid doubts in terms of rights and obligations of the parties, such agreements should be made in writing.

As of 1 January 2017 it is obligatory to keep records of the working time of employees employed on the basis of civil law agreements. Moreover, the minimum hourly rate in 2022 is in this case PLN 19.70 (ca. EUR 4.4).

Provisions of civil law agreements may be defined at the discretion of the parties, based on the Civil Code provisions which apply to different types of agreements; e.g., a contract for specific work should determine a certain result of the work, for example, completion of a given task.

Most often such agreements contain only basic provisions determining the subject matter of the agreement, essential obligations of parties, remuneration, rules for agreement termination, its term, non-competition clauses if any.

Entering into a civil law agreement with a natural person (depending on the kind of agreement and circumstances of its conclusion) may oblige a principal to collect and pay social insurance premiums on the remuneration; e.g., employment under a contract of mandate generally is connected with an obligation to pay some social insurance premiums and the contract for specific work is not connected with such obligation.

8.4. Leased Workers

A leased worker is employed by a temporary employment agency under a term employment contract but works for and under the supervision of another entity (so-called employer-user). The agency may enter into many definite term employment contracts with the same employee. A period of providing work for one employer-user is limited and as a rule is eighteen months at the maximum, within subsequent thirty-six months (if an employee has been employed a few times for shorter periods than eighteen months).

Under the law, a temporary worker may be employed only under certain circumstances, e.g., for seasonal or ad hoc work or to replace an absent worker.

An employer intending to employ a temporary worker has to notify a trade union, if any, of its intention and agree this with the trade union if the planned temporary working time exceeds six months. Rules of law do not regulate such procedure or time within which the trade union should be informed. In practice, information and arrangements should be transferred and made in writing appropriately in advance so that trade unions have time to become familiar with them.

In practice, employment of a temporary worker requires an agreement in writing between an employer-user and temporary employment agency, which should specify in particular a type, period and place of work, working hours and remuneration of the temporary worker.

An employer-user pays the amount due for services to the agency and the agency pays remuneration to the temporary worker.

A temporary worker has analogous obligations as other employees of an employer-user, namely to conscientiously and diligently perform work, follow his/her principal's instructions, obey work regulations, working time and OHS provisions.

Under the law, an employer-user should in particular: ensure safe and hygienic working conditions at a place designated to perform temporary work, keep a record of temporary worker's working time, provide him/her with work clothes, work shoes and protective clothing.

Moreover, an employer-user is obliged to treat a temporary worker in the same manner as it treats employees in terms of working and other employment conditions (in case of breach, a temporary worker has a claim for damages).

Provisions provide for an obligation to grant a temporary worker holiday leave, provided that such a worker has performed work for the same employer-user for at least six months. In the case of damage caused by a temporary worker when performing work, an employer-user may seek redress only from a temporary employment agency.

In the contract with an agency, an employer-user may not commit itself not to employ a temporary worker after the period of temporary work.

8.5. Checklist of Dos and Do Nots

- Make sure that civil law agreement provisions and the manner of rendering services do not contain elements characteristic of the employment relationship.
- Make civil law agreements in writing so as to avoid doubts regarding the rights and obligations of the parties.
- If there is a ban on competition after termination of the civil law agreement, indicate compensation for the period of ban in the agreement.
- Inform a trade union about an intention to employ a temporary worker or agree on this with such union (if a period of temporary employment exceeds six months).

9. OBLIGATION TO BARGAIN COLLECTIVELY WITH TRADE UNIONS: EMPLOYEES' RIGHT TO STRIKE AND A COMPANY'S RIGHT TO CONTINUE BUSINESS OPERATIONS

9.1. Overview of Unions' Right to Organize

Polish law enables free creation and operation of trade unions. The right to create trade unions is vested in all employees (no matter on what basis they are employed) as well as temporary workers and persons working on the basis of civil law agreements (mandate, contract for specific work, management contract) (provided they are not employers). A trade union is established by way of a resolution adopted by at least ten such persons.

The activity of trade unions is not subject to any other entities; they are independent of employers, employers' organizations, state or local authorities.

There is no general list of members of trade unions and employees are not obliged to disclose the fact of being a member of a trade union to their employers. Based on the standpoint of the PPDPO, employee's consent is required for the employer to process data on employee's membership in the trade union. The Trade Union Act allows in certain situations for informing the employer about the employee's membership in a trade union. It is possible when the employer, at the written request of a company's trade union and upon employee's written consent, is obliged to deduct a membership fee from the employee's remuneration in the amount agreed by the employee. However, there were discrepancies in the case law regarding the trade unions obligation to provide a list of all unionized employees upon an employer's request. This matter was resolved at the end of 2012 by a Supreme Court resolution, which represented a pro-union approach and stated that the trade unions are not obliged to provide such a list. The above matter has been confirmed in the judgment of the Supreme Court of 2 April 2019 (I PK 10/18), in which the court found that the refusal to disclose the names and surnames of the members of the company trade union organization to the employer does not deprive this organization of its rights, which depend on the number of members. Moreover, the court indicated that the condition for authentication of establishing a trade union organization and for maintaining its rights was not and is not disclosing the names and surnames of the members of this organization to the employer. Thus, the trade union organization is not obliged to disclose names and surnames of its members to the employer.

In Poland, around 13% of employees are trade union members. Large trade unions are common for employees from various sectors and regions, whereas smaller ones are grouped within a particular sector or within one or more employment establishments. Six per cent belong to the largest trade union NSZZ Solidarność (Independent Self-Governing Trade Union Solidarność, Polish: Niezależny Samorządny Związek Zawodowy Solidarność) and around 3% to the second one OPZZ (National Association of Trade Unions, Polish: Ogólnopolskie Porozumienie Związków Zawodowych).

9.2. Right of Employees to Join Unions

Employees' rights to join, hold and resign from membership of trade unions as well as general regulations on trade unions are regulated in the Trade Union Act.

Each employee and persons employed on the basis of a civil law contract have a right to join a trade union. The statute of a trade union determines membership criteria. Employees may not suffer negative consequences of their (non-) membership of the trade union or fulfilling any function in the trade union. This means that an employer is prohibited from applying any practices which somehow may entail negative (or positive) consequences for employees for their (non-) membership of a trade union. Employees who are trade union activists are specially protected against termination of employment.

9.3. How Employees Select Unions

Employees may freely join any trade union if they meet the requirements set forth in its statute. A trade union may consist of members from one (intra-company trade union) or more employment establishments (intercompany trade union). Trade unions may belong to national associations of trade unions (federations). In turn, national trade unions and associations of trade unions may create national intergroup organizations (confederations). In addition, trade unions, including federations and confederations, may establish and join international employees' organizations.

The elementary duty of a trade union in the employment establishment is to represent interests of employees – trade union members. At the national level, trade unions are entitled to provide their opinions on legal acts, take part in collective disputes and enter into collective bargaining agreements.

Representative trade unions in the meaning of the Act on Tripartite Commission for Social and Economic Affairs and provincial commissions for social dialogue may participate in sessions of the Tripartite Commission and provincial commissions for social dialogue.

In Poland, there are three representative trade union head offices:

(1) Independent Self-Governing Trade Union Solidarność (NSZZ Solidarność). Estimated number of its members is 900,000 grouped in ca. 12,000 company's commissions. Its main bodies are: National Convention of Delegates which meets annually, National Commission and National Audit Commission.
(2) National Association of Trade Unions (OPZZ).
(3) Trade Unions Forum (FZZ) is composed of twenty-seven trade unions representing among others employees from different branches of transport, policemen, nurses and midwives. In total, FZZ has ca. 400,000 members.

Apart from NSZZ Solidarność, OPZZ and FZZ, in Poland there are around 300 federations, 273 national trade unions and around 24,000 local trade unions.

9.4. Pre-election Campaigning

There are no Polish provisions governing the activity of trade unions aimed at acquiring new members. For that purpose, trade unions often organize various promotional and information campaigns.

9.5. Unfair Labour Practices

Practices of treating employees unequally in terms of establishing and terminating employment, terms and conditions of employment, promotion and access to training in order to improve one's professional skills because of (non-) membership of a trade union are tantamount to discrimination. An employee treated unfairly may seek damages equal to at least the minimum remuneration for work (in 2022, it is PLN 3,010–ca. EUR 670).

Moreover, a person who, in connection with his/her position or function held:

(a) Hinders the creation of a trade union compliant with the law.
(b) Hinders activity of a trade union conducted according to the statute.
(c) Discriminates against employees for their (non-)membership of a trade union or for holding a function in the trade union.
(d) Fails to fulfil at least one of the following obligations:
   (i) obligation to inform trade unions active at a company in writing about the transfer of the company to another employer, in particular about the predicted date of transfer, its reasons, legal, economic and social consequences for employees, intended activities regarding employment of such employees as well as obligation to start negotiations with company's trade unions in order to agree on action to be taken by the employer in terms of employment conditions, if the employer intends to take such action;
   (ii) obligation to deduct from the employee's remuneration, at the written request of the trade union and upon the employee's consent, a membership fee in the amount agreed by the employee, and an obligation to immediately transfer such amounts to the bank account indicated by the trade union;
   (iii) obligation to incur costs of employment of an employee released from work for the period of his/her term of office in the intra-company trade union or an employee released from work with a right to remuneration for the period necessary to perform an ad hoc work resulting from his/her function in the trade union if such work may not be performed during his/her free time.
(e) is liable to a fine or restriction of liberty. In most cases, this applies to managerial staff.

9.6. Relocation of Work/Shutdown of Business

Polish law does not define a 'collective dispute'. It is stated that this is a dispute between employees and the employer, and it does not matter how many persons the employer employs. A collective dispute may refer to the following issues: working conditions, salaries, social benefits, rights and freedoms to associate:

- Working conditions.
  'Working conditions' are defined as any circumstances which influence the employee's situation – work environment, work organization, equipment of the employment establishment and social infrastructure at the employment establishment.
- Salaries.
- Social benefits.
  'Social benefits' cover living, housing and cultural needs of employees such as living, housing and employment conditions, education, work protection, social security, health protection, welfare, protection of the handicapped, using one's free time.
- Rights and freedoms to associate.

If a collective dispute relating to the above working conditions is not resolved within negotiations or mediation, employees may go on strike. A strike may only refer to matters covered by a collective dispute. Employees whose work is connected with ensuring safety to people may not go on strike.

Employee's participation in an organized strike in compliance with the Act on resolving collective disputes does not breach employees' obligations. Within a period of strike organized in compliance with the law, an employee retains a right to social insurance benefits and rights under an employment relationship, except for remuneration. The period of break in work is included in the period of employment at a workplace.

9.7. Checklist of Dos and Do Nots

- Do not impede employees' participation in the trade union, in particular, do not discriminate against them because of that.
- Offer trade unions premises and facilities (such as telephone, computer, fax) in order to carry out trade union activity.
- Agree or consult with trade unions on all issues regarding pay and working conditions.

10. WORKING CONDITIONS: HOURS OF WORK AND PAYMENT OF WAGES – BY STATUTE OR COLLECTIVE AGREEMENTS

10.1. Overview of Wage and Hours Laws

A general rule provides for eight-hour working time, which is on average forty hours in the average five-day working week in a given settlement period which should not exceed four months.

Apart from a basic working time system, there are also:

- equivalent working time in which a daily working time (eight hours in the basic system) may be extended to a maximum of twelve hours a day. Longer working time within one day means that employee's working time in another day must be shortened so that within the settlement period which, in this system lasts for one month, the above general limits are not exceeded;
- interrupted working time during which in each twenty-four-hour period one maximum five-hour long break may be established;
- task-based working time applies mainly to persons in charge of the company and managerial staff;
- flexible forms of working time such as shortened working week, shortened working time and weekend system of working time.

The basic document regulating conditions for remuneration is a collective bargaining agreement. It is concluded by an employer (employers) and trade unions. There are two types of such agreements, namely intra-company (referring to one employer) and intercompany (covering in principle all employers belonging to the organization which entered into a given agreement).

If an employer employs more than fifty people not covered by any collective bargaining agreement, the employer is obliged to determine remuneration conditions in the remuneration regulations. This number refers to all employees irrespective of the basis on which they are employed and whether they are full-time or part-time workers.

10.2. Minimum Wage

In Poland, the minimum wage is set forth annually in a regulation of the Council of Ministers. Each year such a regulation shall be issued before 15 September. In 2022 the minimum wage amounts to PLN 3,010 gross (ca. EUR 670).

10.3. Overtime

Overtime is allowed only in a certain amount and need to be compensated – not only with standard remuneration but also with a certain additional amount.

Overtime is permissible only in case of emergencies, during a rescue action and other similar cases as well as due to the special needs of the employer.

The basic term used to determine overtime is a '24-hour work cycle' beginning from the time when the employee starts work on a given day. As a result, each additional hour beyond the working time of a given employee within such twenty-four hours is considered an overtime hour.

There is also an annual limit of overtime hours of 150. This number may be modified in collective bargaining agreements, regulations and employment contract. However, this may not exceed eight overtime hours per week.

For overtime, apart from regular remuneration, the following allowance shall be due: 100% for overtime performed, e.g., at night, on Sundays and legal holidays and 50% on any other day.

Additionally, provisions do not enable all employees to work overtime. It is prohibited, e.g., for pregnant women and minor employees.

The Labour Code provides for the possibility of prolonging the maximum settlement period of working hours from four to twelve months in every working time system, provided that the following conditions are fulfilled:

- the existence of the objective or technological reasons or reasons referring to the organization of the working time;
- the procedure of introducing in the collective labour agreement with the company trade union organization or in the work regulations agreed with such organization. If there is no company trade union organization operating within the particular employer, then the prolongation must be in agreement with the employees' representatives chosen pursuant to the procedure adopted within such employer.

This solution makes it possible to safeguard jobs and prevent employee dismissals during periods of general economic slowdown or as a result of the individual difficulties faced by entrepreneurs.

The employer is obliged to provide the distribution of working time in writing or electronically for a period shorter than a settlement period but covering at least one month. The employer must inform the employee of his/her current working time schedule one week before he/she is set to commence work.

The employer does not have to make the distribution if:

- employee work time is derived from the employment contract, collective labour agreement, work regulations or notice;
- the employee individually agreed with the employer on the time necessary to perform entrusted tasks;
- the employee submitted a written request to the employer to apply variable working hours;
- the employee submitted a written request to the employer to apply a flexible work schedule.

The introduction of variable working hours means that:

- the employee's work schedule may provide different hours for starting work;
- the employer may set the time interval in which the employee himself or herself can decide the starting time for their work;
- redoing work on the same twenty-four-hour work cycle will not involve the employee working overtime.

The variable working hours cannot affect the right of an employee to eleven hours of uninterrupted rest each day and a period of thirty-five hours of uninterrupted rest each week.

The employee has the right to submit a written request to the employer for time off to settle personal matters. If the employer agrees to provide the employee time off for this purpose, the period during which the employee works off such exemption will not be treated as overtime.

10.4. Meal and Rest Periods

Under the Labour Code, if an employee works for at least six hours, he/she is entitled to a break of at least fifteen minutes included in the working time. This does not refer to a working time resulting from the working time system and schedule, but the time during which he/she really worked.

Moreover, an employer may introduce one maximum sixty-minute break, which will not be calculated as a working time.

The basic requirement within a twenty-four-hour cycle is to guarantee an employee at least eleven hours of uninterrupted rest in each such cycle. This regulation does not apply to employees who manage on behalf of an employer a company, and when it is necessary to carry out a rescue action in order to protect human life or health, property or environment or to remove a failure. It does not mean that such employees do not need to be guaranteed rest of proper duration. The employer is obliged to plan the working time so that such employees are ensured an equivalent amount of rest within a certain settlement period.

Another limitation in planning a working time by an employer is a requirement to ensure employees an uninterrupted rest of thirty-five hours each week. This regulation also differs with regard to employees managing on behalf of the employer the employment establishment, and to cases when it is necessary to carry out a rescue action in order to save human life or health, protect property or environment and remove a failure. For that category of employees, a weekly uninterrupted rest may be shorter; however, it may not be shorter than twenty-four hours.

10.5. Deductions from Wages

Detailed regulations regarding deductions from remuneration and maximum amounts of such deductions constitute one of the elements of remuneration protection. Without the employee's consent, only deductions listed in the Labour Code may be made. Provisions allow for deductions of dues resulting from:

- cash advances given to an employee, and
- cash penalties imposed on the employee for breaching OHS provisions or fire regulations, unjustified absence from work, coming to work intoxicated or drinking alcohol at work.

10.6. Garnishment

Except for deductions set forth in section 10.5 above, it is possible to make deductions of dues resulting from:

- maintenance benefits enforced under enforcement titles;
- other dues than maintenance benefits enforced under enforcement titles.

Deductions are made in a certain order (first maintenance and financial penalties imposed by the employer as the last) and only within limits specified in the provisions. It is not allowed to exceed the non-deductible amount.

10.7. Exemptions to Wage and Hour Laws

Some labour law provisions provide for exemptions for certain employee groups.

Managerial staff is entitled to receive remuneration and addition only for overtime hours on Sunday or bank holiday provided that no day free of work is guaranteed instead. Such employees are not entitled to benefits for the below-mentioned duty.

Also, when an employee is on duty and remains ready to work beyond his/her standard working hours, this does not entitle him/her to receive compensation as he/she would receive for overtime hours. Home duty does not entail any additional benefits, but duty served at another place entitles to time off (corresponding to the duration of duty), and if it is not possible to grant time off, to be given compensation.

If managerial staff work overtime permanently, they are also entitled to overtime pay for work performed on other days than Sunday and bank holidays.

10.8. Child Labour

Under Polish law, the ability to work is granted to persons who attained 18 years. The work of minors is always treated as exceptional and is specially protected. With regard to children, there are two categories for which work is treated differently.

Minor employees are between 15 and 18 years, and they may perform work only under certain conditions, which are as follows:

- 15 years of age;
- graduating from primary school (*szkoła podstawowa*);
- medical certificate confirming that work to be performed does not threaten the minor's health.

However, children (namely those below 15 years of age) may provide work only exceptionally and for certain entities – those who carry out cultural, artistic, sport or advertising activity. Moreover, prior consent of a statutory representative or guardian of a child and labour inspector's permit is required.

10.9. Record-Keeping Requirements

10.9.1. Information That Must Be Maintained

Based on provisions, each employer, regardless of its activity or level of employment, is obliged to keep a record of working time. Such record should be kept separately for each employee and include both the working time (including overtime) and free time (including leave and other justified absence from work).

10.9.2. Records That Must Be Retained

Documentation regarding employees must be stored for ten years.

10.9.3. Failure to Maintain Required Records

Failure to maintain required records constitutes an offence against employee's rights and is punishable with a fine from PLN 1,000 (ca. EUR 222) to PLN 30,000 (ca. EUR 6,670).

It may also entail negative consequences when the employee raises a claim for remuneration for overtime hours. If the employer does not provide evidence, the court will rely on the employee's assertions and presented proofs, such as calendars.

10.10. Reductions in Compensation Caused by Economic Downturn

If required by the financial situation of the employer (provisions do not specify conditions to be met), it is possible to enter into an agreement on less favourable employment conditions for employees than the current ones for a temporary period. This also applies to remuneration. The maximum period for which such an agreement may be binding is three years.

10.11. Checklist of Dos and Do Nots

- Determine remuneration rules but observe equal treatment rules.
- Keep a record of working time of employees, including overtime.
- Pay for overtime hours in compliance with binding law.
- Deduct from remuneration only amounts permitted by law.

11. OTHER WORKING CONDITIONS AND BENEFITS: BY STATUTE, COLLECTIVE AGREEMENTS OR COMPANY POLICY

11.1. Health and Other Insurance

From the day of commencing work, all employees are covered by social insurance, namely retirement, disability, sickness, accident and health insurance.

Social insurance premiums are paid by an employer who pays part of premiums from its own means, and the other part is deducted from the employee's remuneration.

11.2. Pension and Retirement Benefits

According to the law, the retirement age is 60 for women and 65 for men. The amount of pension depends on the length of service and on the amounts of premiums paid during employment. Pension is paid by the Social Insurance Authority. An employer is not obliged to pay any part of the pension to an employee.

The employer is only obliged to pay a retiring employee so-called retirement severance pay equal to one month's remuneration unless internal regulations provide for a higher amount.

11.2.1. Employee Capital Plans

Definition of PPK

Employee capital plans (PPK) are savings schemes which are mandatory for employers and voluntary for employees. Each month, a certain percentage of the employee's remuneration is transferred to a special account of a financial institution with which the employer has concluded a contract for the management of PPK. This capital will be entirely owned by the employee.

Persons Covered by the PPK

PPK are created by employers obligatorily for employees and persons employed on the basis of civil law contracts. Persons between the age of 18 and 55 will be enrolled automatically in the PPK and persons between the age of 55 and 70 will be enrolled voluntarily at their request; however, the employer must inform them about this possibility. An employee may at any time resign from participation in the PPK.

Financing of PPK and Costs

The basic payments to the fund are made by both the employer and the employee:

- mandatory payments from an employee amount to 2% of the monthly gross remuneration, and additional voluntary contributions up to 2% of the monthly gross remuneration;
- obligatory payments from the employer amount to 1.5% of the monthly gross remuneration of the concerned employee, and additional voluntary payments up to 2.5% of the monthly gross remuneration of the employee concerned. The payments of the employee will be an additional cost on the employer's side.

Timetable for the Introduction of PPK

The obligation to comply with the Act on PPK has been introduced gradually:

- from 1 July 2019 for entities that employ at least 250 people as of 31 December 2018;
- from 1 January 2020 for entities employing at least 50 people as of 30 June 2019;
- from 1 July 2020 for entities employing at least 20 persons as of 31 December 2019;
- from 1 January 2021 for other entities employing up to 19 employees and public sector employing entities.

11.3. Vacation and Holiday Payments on Termination

An employee finishing work at a given employer may use its holiday during notice period, provided that an employer consents to this. If the employer does not grant holiday to the employee during the notice period or if such holiday entitlement is longer than the notice period, the employer is obliged to pay an equivalent for unused holiday. In addition, if a notice period lasts for at least two weeks and it was the employer who terminated employment, the employee is entitled to two or three days off work to search for new work. The employee receives remuneration for those days off work.

An employer is entitled to unilaterally release an employee from the duty to report to work during their notice period while the employee retains the right for remuneration, regardless of the type of employment contract.

11.4. Leaves of Absence

11.4.1. Personal Leave

The number of days of personal leave depends on the employee's length of service. The length of service also includes education; i.e., graduation from studies is equal to eight years. A person with more than ten years of employment is entitled to twenty-six days of leave within a year, and a person who has fewer than ten years of employment may use twenty days of leave. In order to be granted leave, an employee has to apply for it (most often in the form of application for leave), and the employer may, but does not have to, grant such leave. An employee may not waive his/her right to leave and should use it within a given calendar year, but no later than 30 September of the following year.

11.4.2. Medical or Sick Leave

In the case of illness, an employee is entitled to sick leave. Upon presenting a medical certificate an employee is released from work within a given period. During illness, an employee retains his/her right to remuneration and then to sickness benefit (sometimes in full and sometimes in reduced amount).

For the first thirty-three days of employee's sickness within a calendar year (for the first fourteen days for employees over fifty), the employer pays remuneration of 80% (100% in the case of sickness during pregnancy or accident on the way to/from work). Remuneration for each following day of excused absence from work is paid by the Social Insurance Authority from social insurance resources (sickness benefit).

11.4.3. Bereavement Leave

In the event of death of an employee's relative, an employee has a right to be released from work. Depending on the degree of kinship with the deceased, an employee is entitled to one day off (death of a sister, brother, mother-in-law, father-in-law, grandmother, grandfather or employee's dependent or person under the direct care of an employee) or two days off (death of employee's spouse or child, father, mother, stepfather or stepmother).

11.4.4. Family Leave

An employee may be released from work in the event of his/her wedding or birth of his/her child (two days) and the wedding of his/her child (one day).

11.4.5. Pregnancy Leave

Part of maternity leave (referred to in section 11.4.6. below) may fall due prior to the predicted childbirth date. Then the length of maternity leave is shortened by the already used part.

11.4.6. Maternity Leave

An employee who gave birth to a child is entitled to maternity leave. The length of maternity leave depends on the number of children born and is twenty weeks for one child and is extended gradually up to thirty-seven weeks for quintuplets (or more children).

Once the maternity leave comes to an end, one of the parents, upon a motion submitted to the employer, is entitled to an additional thirty-two or thirty-four weeks of parental leave, depending on the number of children born. During the maternity leave and first six to eight weeks of the parental leave (depending on the number of children born or whether the leave was taken due to adoption), the maternity benefit would be paid in the full amount, whereas during the rest of the leave only 60% of the benefit would be paid, unless the motion for the parental leave would be submitted within twenty-one days after the childbirth. In such a case, the maternity leave and the parental leave would be paid at the level of 80%.

The parents are entitled to childcare leave which amounts to thirty-six months and could be used in any proportion by both parents. Within the limit indicated above, both parents are entitled to one month of leave non-transferable to the partner, which means that if one partner does not use the month to which they are individually entitled, it will be lost. The leave is not paid. There is also the possibility of dividing the leave into a maximum of five parts. The leave can be used until the child is 6 years old.

11.4.7. Injury at Work

Work accident injury insurance is one of the integral components of social insurance which covers each employee from the day of employment until employment termination.

The amount of monthly premiums paid by the employer for work accident injury insurance is from 0.40% to 8.12% of monthly employee's revenue.

Work accident injury insurance premiums are paid in total by an employer. An employer is also obliged to submit monthly reports for each employee to the Social Insurance Authority with a list of due social insurance premiums.

11.5. Checklist of Dos and Do Nots

- If you do not want to pay a holiday payment, oblige the employee in the termination letter to use his/her outstanding holiday in the notice period.
- Remember to oblige the employee to use his/her holiday by 30 September of the following year at the latest.

12. WORKERS' COMPENSATION

12.1. Overview

Polish law provides for the general obligation of some employers to maintain a social benefit fund, aimed to finance benefits for current and retired employees, as well as their families. Amounts of the fund are managed by the employer and kept in a separate bank account.

In principle the obligation to set up the social benefit fund depends on the headcount in the company as of 1 January each year; i.e., employers hiring at least fifty employees (calculated per full-time positions) need to set up the fund.

Smaller employers can set up the fund voluntarily; however, they need to inform employees that the fund will not be set up, by the end of January in a given year, in accordance with the practice adopted at the workplace (e.g., information on a notice board or delivered and confirmed by each employee).

Employers' commencing activity during the calendar year, covered by the fund obligation, should make payments to the fund as of the subsequent calendar year. If, however, commencement of the activity was a result of, e.g., acquisition of at least fifty employees, the fund should be set up immediately.

Employers obliged to set up the fund can be released from that obligation upon the consent of representatives of the staff (trade unions or employee appointed by the staff). The relevant provisions should be included in the collective bargaining agreement or remuneration regulations.

The payments to the fund need to be made annually, in two instalments:

(1) 75% of the due amount by 31 May; and
(2) 25% of the due amount by 30 September.

The due amount is calculated as a percentage of an average monthly remuneration in Poland for the previous year, per average headcount at the employer. In 2022, the basic amount is PLN 1,550.26 (ca. EUR 344) per employee (remaining at the same level as in 2020). Collective bargaining agreement can set the aforesaid amounts differently.

Benefits from the fund are granted discretionally, but on the basis of social criteria, i.e., taking into account if, e.g., an employee suffered a prolonged illness, an accident or took care of disabled family members.

Specific criteria and principles of granting the benefits should be set out in the social benefit fund regulation, agreed by the employer with the trade unions (if any) or with a representative elected by the employees.

Employees sent by the employer to a different city, or a place which is not the regular place of work under the employment contract, are entitled to receive business trip allowance as well as additionally reimbursement of expenses related to the trip (e.g., travel, accommodation, local transport, use of employee's car for the trip).

Conditions of payment of the allowance and the reimbursement are specified in statutory provisions, which are generally applicable to all employers. More favourable conditions can be stipulated in the collective bargaining agreement, remuneration regulations or employment contract.

12.2. Checklist of Dos and Do Nots

- If the headcount is less than fifty employees per full-time positions and you do not intend to establish a social benefit fund or pay the holiday benefit in a given year, make sure to inform employees about this, by the end of January in a given year, in accordance with the practice adopted at the workplace (e.g., information on a notice board or delivered to each employee) and keep the record of this.
- Keep the deadlines for payments to the social benefit fund.

13. COMPANY'S OBLIGATION TO PROVIDE SAFE AND HEALTHY WORKPLACE

13.1. Overview of Safety and Environmental Laws and Regulations

Safety and environmental provisions in Polish law are generally stipulated in the Labour Code and numerous executive regulations concerning, e.g., specific industries and professions.

The law provides for numerous obligations of employers, such as ensuring safe and hygienic work conditions for employees and arranging the work accordingly, providing relevant work safety training, as well as responsibilities (which cannot be transferred to third parties or employees) for the condition of the work premises, sanitary facilities, machines, tools and equipment used by the employees, as well as for the choice of technological processes and chemicals used in the work process. Moreover, the financial situation does not exempt employers from the performance of the aforesaid duties. The jurisprudence of the Polish Supreme Court states that employers are obliged not only to fulfil requirements but foremost to ensure actual safety of the staff.

13.2. Requirements

13.2.1. General Obligations

Under the Labour Code, the employer's general obligations related to providing a safe and healthy workplace include: ensuring safe and hygienic working conditions, holding regular training for employees on safe and hygienic work, financing medical tests for each employee and directing each employee to such tests.

13.2.2. Providing Information

It is also required to inform employees about life and health hazards at the workplace, and on each job position, as well as on the relevant protocols of conduct in the event of breakdowns or other hazardous situations (among others concerning protective and preventive measures aimed to eliminate or limit the hazards).

The staff needs to be also informed about employees competent for rendering first aid, as well as for firefighting and evacuations, their place of work, phone numbers or e-mails. Such competent employees should be appointed by the employer and need to have relevant training organized at the employer's cost.

Moreover, employees need to be immediately informed about potential life and health hazards and provided with the instructions facilitating leaving the endangered premises. If the hazard actually takes place, it is necessary to instruct the staff to stop working and move to a safe location.

13.2.3. First Aid and Fires

Employers need to make sure that there are first aid kits and points and fire extinguishers at the workplace as well as other equipment necessary for rendering help in case of accidents, fires or evacuations.

If the situation involves work of personnel hired by two or more employers at the same location (e.g., on a construction site), such employers are required to cooperate in order to ensure compliance with relevant OHS regulations. Cooperation requires appointing a coordinator supervising the OHS of all employees, setting cooperation rules of conduct in case of life and health hazards (including, e.g., exchange of information or rendering first aid) as well as informing each other and the employees on relevant preventive measures.

13.2.4. Work Health and Safety Employees or Service

If there are up to 100 employees at the workplace, an employer should appoint one of the employees (who underwent training and has experience in OHS matters) to perform advisory and control functions in terms of OHS in addition to his/her regular obligations. This includes control of conditions of work and compliance with the relevant regulations, informing the employer about discovered infringements or hazards, as well as providing the employer, at least once a year, with analysis of OHS conditions and suggestions thereto. Employers hiring more than 100 employees should appoint a work health and safety service instead, which is competent for tasks in the aforesaid scope and composed of at least one employee (having relevant training and experience) whose work will be entirely devoted to the issue of OHS at the workplace. Alternatively, an employer can entrust the aforesaid tasks to external service providers with relevant training and experience, specializing in OHS issues, if there are no employees at the workplace who have qualifications in these matters.

Irrespectively of appointing the work health and safety service, employers hiring more than 250 employees are obliged to appoint a work health and safety commission which serves as an advisory and consultative body, composed of an equal number of representatives of employer and employees (appointed by the trade unions or, if there are none, by the employees according to internal practice at the workplace). Its tasks include, among others, review and evaluation of working conditions, as well as cooperating with the employer in the scope of compliance with OHS obligations.

13.3. Rights of Employees

All employees are entitled to safe and hygienic working conditions, which need to be ensured by an employer, as well as to receive training concerning the OHS rules during the working time, financed by an employer.

In the event that working conditions contravene the provisions of law and simultaneously pose a direct threat to the health and life of the staff, employees may abstain from work, notifying the supervisor forthwith. If refraining from work is not sufficient to move aside an immediate danger to life or health, an employee may leave the endangered place and notify his/her supervisor. This may not deteriorate the employee's situation or affect his/her right to remuneration for that period.

Moreover, an employee is generally entitled to abstain from work which requires special psychophysical abilities (e.g., air traffic controllers or operators of cranes) where his/her health condition does not ensure safe work performance and poses a threat to others. This, however, does not apply to employees whose work obligations include saving life or property, for example, doctors or nurses.

Employees' rights include receiving information on occupational hazard related to their work and on respective principles of protection as well as receiving protective wear or workwear if required for the performance of work.

13.4. Rights of Employer

In general, the OHS regulations provide for obligations rather than the rights of the employer. Such rights can be derived from the employer's obligations; for example, the right to control the compliance with OHS provisions at the workplace results from the obligation to ensure safety at the workplace. Moreover, the employer can request that employees comply with the relevant provisions of the OHS (e.g., use of workwear), request fulfilment of relevant obligations by employees, or apply penalties for violations of the aforesaid provision (e.g., impose a reprimand) and in extreme cases terminate the employment of violators.

13.5. Specific Standards

Polish law provides for certain requirements and standards of OHS, which are generally regulated in the Labour Code and specifically stipulated in a number of executive regulations, concerning specific issues related to various aspects of employment matters, types of work or industries.

Employer needs to ensure that buildings and premises in which the work is (or will be) performed and their condition comply with OHS standards, in particular ensuring that work premises are adequate to the type of work and headcount.

Polish law provides for employers' obligations related to preventive health care, including in particular evaluation of occupational risks, informing employees about them and about protective measures, conducting studies and measurements aimed at preventing occupational illnesses and eliminating hazardous factors, as well as keeping relevant records. All employees need to undergo pre-employment medical tests as well as periodical and control tests. If the result of the test proves that an employee is unable to work at the current position, the employer needs to move the employee to a different position and, if this is connected with salary reduction, pay compensatory remuneration for up to six months.

Training

In general prior to work commencement and periodically, the employee needs to take part in OHS training held within his/her working time and financed by the employer. Frequency of training depends on the type of work.

13.6. Injury or Accident at Work

Polish law defines an accident at work as a sudden event which results in injury or death, is caused by an external source (i.e., a situation independent of the employee) and connected with the work (during performance of work as well as during a period in which an employee is ready to work, e.g., on the way to/from work). The accident is considered fatal if it causes an employee's death within six months from the date of accident, or serious if it causes serious injuries such as sight loss or incapacity to work, or a group accident if it is caused by the same event and affects at least two persons.

According to the Polish Labour Code, in the event of an accident the employer is required to appoint an investigative body which should immediately look into the circumstances and causes of the accident, and in particular, determine if the accident is connected with the performance of work.

An employer is also obliged to notify each fatal, serious or group accident at work (including accidents which may subsequently result in death or serious injury of one or more employees) to the competent National Labour Inspector and a competent public prosecutor, as well as keep a record of accidents at work and records of investigations of the accidents for a period of ten years.

13.7. Workplace Violence

The issue of violence at the workplace is not specifically regulated in Polish labour law. Obligations of employers in this respect are derived from general regulations on ensuring a safe work environment and protecting the life and health of employees, as well as regulations concerning the prevention of mobbing and abuse at the workplace. Employers often adopt anti-mobbing or anti-discrimination policies which specify codes of conduct for employees in such cases. Moreover, according to the judgments of the Polish Supreme Court, physical violence at the workplace may justify the immediate dismissal of an employee – the offender.

13.8. Fines and Penalties

There are several penalties provided for in the statutory regulations, which can be applied by state courts or the National Labour Inspectorate in cases of violation of obligations related to OHS.

Any persons responsible for safety and hygiene at the workplace (e.g., employer, person acting on behalf of the employer, employee working in the internal work health and safety service) and persons managing employees (e.g., department manager, foreman) are generally responsible for ensuring compliance with relevant OHS provisions and obligations. In case of infringements, the aforesaid persons may be penalized with a fine from PLN 1,000 to PLN 30,000 (ca. EUR 222–EUR 6,670). In the event that infringements are life-threatening or may cause serious health deterioration, the person responsible can be penalized with a fine form PLN 100 up to PLN 1,080.000 (ca. EUR 22–EUR 240,000.), limitation of freedom, e.g., community work (from one month up to twelve months) or imprisonment (from one month up to three years).

13.9. Checklists of Dos and Do Nots

- Make sure to comply with general provisions of OHS and provisions applicable to your type of business or industry (if any).
- Arrange medical tests and training for employees.
- Appoint employees competent for rendering first aid, firefighting and evacuations.
- Comply with the requirements related to work health and safety service; i.e., appoint an employee or a body, or entrust these tasks to a professional service provider.
- Appoint a work health and safety commission if the headcount reaches 250 employees.
- Make sure that employees comply with OHS provisions.

14. IMMIGRATION, SECONDMENT AND FOREIGN ASSIGNMENT

14.1. Overview Laws Controlling Immigration

The European Union/European Economic Area (EU/EEA) citizens can commence employment in Poland without obtaining a work permit. However, if their stay in Poland exceeds three months, they have to register with the foreigners' department of a provincial office (*urząd wojewódzki*) competent for the place of their stay. The EU/EEA nationals can generally either commence employment in Poland on their own or be posted/seconded to work in Poland by employers in their home countries. In principle, employees from the EU/EEA Member States must be treated at least in the same way as Polish employees, but they also need to comply with Polish employment regulations. For further information in this respect *see* section 14.5.

Under Polish law employees from countries other than EU/EEA Member States are generally obliged to obtain a work permit, issued by the province governor (*wojewoda*) upon application of the employer, provided that the third-country nationals: (i) will be employed in Poland by a Polish employer; (ii) will reside in Poland for a total period of over six months during subsequent twelve months, in connection with membership of a management board of, e.g., a company registered in Poland; or (iii) will work in Poland on the basis of posting or secondment by their foreign employer to work, e.g., at a Polish subsidiary for a total period of over thirty days during the calendar year, to temporarily perform services in Poland, or work in Poland for a total period of over thirty days during subsequent six months.

The procedure for obtaining work permits usually consists of two steps: first, the employee applies for documents legalizing his/her stay in Poland in connection with the performance of work (e.g., employment visa, residence permit). Second, the employer who is hiring or posting/seconding a foreigner to work in Poland applies for a work permit.

A work permit does not guarantee a freedom of movement on the Polish labour market, but (with minor exceptions) only allows the performance of a specific type of work or a given position during a defined period. Depending on the type of work permit, this period may be up to three or five years and may also be extended. In practice, the provincial offices grant the first work permit for a shorter period, e.g., the Provincial Office in Warsaw grants the first work permit for one year only.

Polish law stipulates specific requirements for hiring foreigners, which differ if, for example, a foreigner is employed directly by a Polish employer, or posted to work in Poland by a foreign employer. In general Polish employers who decide to hire foreigners first need to search the local labour market for possible candidates and obtain information from the local employment office in this respect, before submitting an application for a work permit for foreigners.

However, citizens of six Eastern European countries (covering citizens of Armenia, Belarus, Georgia, Moldova, Russia or Ukraine) may be employed based on a simplified procedure. They may perform work for a period of six months in the next twelve months without the need to obtain a work permit, provided that they have a written declaration of the entity entrusting the performance of work, registered in the relevant district labour office and a written contract. In a situation where the employer wants to employ a foreigner for a longer period of time, a work permit or a temporary residence and work permit or a temporary residence permit to perform work in a profession requiring high qualifications is required. If a foreigner worked for a given employer in connection with a registered declaration, that employer may apply for a work permit (for the same position) in a simplified mode (without the need to obtain information about the inability to meet the employer's staffing needs on the local labour market).

There is also a new solution enabling the employment of foreigners in Poland for seasonal work – which introduces the possibility of a seasonal work permit. Seasonal work means work performed for a period not longer than nine months in a calendar year in the sectors of agriculture, horticulture, tourism – as part of activities considered to be seasonal. In this aspect, there are again some advantages for the citizens of Armenia, Belarus, Georgia, Moldova, Russia and Ukraine. In case the employer employs foreigners from above six countries, he does not need to include information about the inability to meet the employer's staffing needs on the local labour market when applying for a seasonal work permit. The employer can also apply for issuing the so-called multi-season permit, if:

- the employer wants to systematically employ foreigners from above six countries for seasonal work,
- in the period of five years preceding the date of submitting the application, the employer entrusted the work to a foreigner based on a seasonal work permit at least once.

In this case, the district head (*starosta*) may enter the application in the register of applications for a seasonal work permit for periods not longer than nine months in a calendar year, within no more than three consecutive calendar years.

The employer can also entrust a citizen of Armenia, Belarus, Georgia, Moldova, Russia or Ukraine, during the period of validity of their seasonal work permit (except for temporary workers), other work than seasonal work, for a period of up to thirty days, without the need to apply for a separate work permit. However, in such a situation the foreigner must be provided with remuneration at least in the same amount as specified in the seasonal work permit.

It should be borne in mind that this permit does not grant the foreigner the right of access to the Polish labour market (it is only in connection with the seasonal work).

There are also numerous cases in which foreigners from Third Countries are allowed to work in Poland without a work permit (e.g., foreign language teachers working in schools, university students working in summer, provided that their stay has a legal basis).

Due to the ongoing warfare in Ukraine, Poland introduced on 12 March Law on Assistance to Citizens of Ukraine, which comprises, *inter alia*, special employment provisions. Thus Ukrainian nationals may participate in the Polish labour market in principle in the same way as Polish nationals do, provided that their stay in Poland is legal (regardless of specific legal basis). The sole condition to be met is their registration in the local labour office by their employee in fourteen days from entrusting work. The registration is not obligatory if the Ukrainian national already could take up work without permit based on preexisting legislation. However, once the special act is revoked regular provisions will apply, unless there is new legislation in place.

14.2. Recruiting, Screening and Hiring Process

There are no general requirements for recruiting, screening and hiring process of foreigners who obtained a work permit. However, if Polish employers wish to hire foreigners directly, they have to check with the local employment office if there are potential candidates for the position offered to a foreigner on the local labour market unless work entrusted to a foreigner is on the list of jobs which do not require such prior check. Lists are set by each province governor. Moreover, remuneration of a foreigner needs to be set by the Polish employer in an amount not lower than the remuneration of employees holding a similar position, or performing comparable work.

14.3. Obligation of Employer to Enforce Immigration Laws

The employer is obliged to comply with the relevant immigration laws. This includes an obligation to observe requirements for obtaining a work permit or other obligations under the law. Compliance with immigration laws can be checked by the National Labour Inspectorate by way of control of the employer. Moreover, it is necessary to inform the competent provincial office which has issued a work permit if a foreigner has not commenced employment within three months from the date of validity of the work permit or if the foreigner has ended performance of work earlier than three months prior to the expiry of the permit.

14.4. Fines and Penalties

Hiring foreigners without the required work permit may lead to a fine of at least PLN 1,000 and up to PLN 30,000 (ca. EUR 222–EUR 6,670) which is imposed on the person responsible for hiring a foreigner. If the illegal employment involves, e.g., forcing foreigners to work, the fine can amount to up to PLN 30,000 (ca. EUR 6,670). On the other hand, foreigners who illegally perform work are subject to a fine of at least PLN 20 and up to PLN 5,000 (ca. EUR 4.00–EUR 1,111). A fine of PLN 100 to PLN 5,000 (ca. EUR 21 – EUR 1,111) may be imposed on the person responsible for hiring a foreigner in case of failure to comply with the obligation to notify the province governor (*wojewoda*) in writing about entrusting a foreigner with work.

The breach of the law will also be notified to the police or Border Guard. This may result in the expulsion of a foreigner, and in such a case, relevant costs shall be borne by the employer or the person who entrusted a foreigner with a job.

14.5. Secondment/Foreign Assignment

When posting/assigning foreign employees (from the EU/EEA and the Third Countries) to work in Poland, their conditions of employment should be as favourable as the conditions of employment resulting from Polish employment law.

According to the new provisions on the posting/assigning of employees (which entered into force on 4 September 2020) an employer posting an employee to the territory of the Republic of Poland, within a period of up to twelve months of posting to work in Poland, is obliged to provide him/her with appropriate employment conditions, guaranteeing minimum protection, resulting from the provisions of the Labour Code and other provisions regulating the rights and obligations of employees. This includes in particular working time standards, amount of working time and daily and weekly rest periods, length of holiday leave, remuneration for work (covering all mandatory remuneration components, including an allowance for overtime work), work safety and hygiene standards, protection of pregnant employees and employees during maternity leave, employment of young people, the principle of equal treatment and the prohibition of discrimination in employment, as well as receivables to cover the costs related to a business trip from the place of work in the territory of Poland, to which the employee was posted, to another place of work on or outside the territory of Poland.

According to the new provisions on the posting/assigning of employees, the secondment period has been reduced to twelve months. However, this period may be extended by six months (up to eighteen months in total), provided that the employer submits an empowered notification to the National Labour Inspectorate (a letter motivating the need to provide work after the secondment period of twelve months).

Thus, when the actual posting/assigning period exceeds twelve months, the employer may:

- provide the employee with a broader scope of employment conditions than the minimum terms stipulated in the act, or
- submit reasoned notifications and be entitled to extend the application of the minimum employment conditions until the end of the eighteen-month posting period.

Furthermore, based on new provisions, the periods of posting/assigning employees will be added together – thus, the posting/assigning period shall mean the total duration of the posting/assigning periods of individual posted employees performing the same task at the same place. The above aims to ensure that the replacements for posted employees are not used to circumvent the rules on the posting of employees in the framework of the provision of services. Moreover, the foreign employer is obliged to appoint a representative in contacts with the National Labour Inspectorate (such representative must be in Poland during the period of posting). The foreign employee is also obliged to submit certain data to the National Labour Inspectorate (e.g., name of the posted employee, planned date of commencement and end of work of the posted employee, type of work, etc.). The employer must store the following documents (in paper or electronic version): (i) copy of the employment agreement with the posted employee; (ii) documents concerning the posted employee's working time; and (iii) documents concerning the posted employee's remuneration. The above-mentioned documents may be written in a language other than Polish; however, within five days from the National Labour Inspectorate's request, a Polish translation must be submitted.

When posting/assigning Polish employees to work in the EU Member States, the Polish employer needs to ensure working conditions as favourable as conditions resulting from provisions of local law. If posting/assignment entails work in a third country for a period exceeding one month, Polish employers need to specify in the employment contract a period of assignment and the currency in which the remuneration will be paid, as well as inform the employee in writing about any benefits related to foreign assignment (including reimbursement of expenses related to transport to the country of destination and accommodation), as well as about any changes in this respect.

14.6. Checklist of Dos and Do Nots

- Make sure that the third-country foreigner has an employment visa or another document enabling him/her to arrive at or stay in Poland before processing with an application for a work permit.
- Note that an application for a work permit needs to be filed by the employer and not by the foreign employee.
- Review relevant work permit requirements applicable to the employment of foreigners in Poland (e.g., assignment to work in a subsidiary).
- Comply with the requirements related to terms and conditions of employment of employees posted/assigned abroad either within or outside the EU/EEA.
- Make sure that the EU/EEA nationals comply with residence registration requirements if they stay in Poland for more than three months.

15. RESTRICTIVE COVENANTS AND PROTECTION OF TRADE SECRETS AND CONFIDENTIAL INFORMATION

15.1. Overview

Employees' obligations regarding the protection of trade secrets and confidential information can be derived from statutory provisions of the Labour Code or the Act on combating unfair competition. However, the commendable practice of employers is to specify confidentiality obligations in employment contracts or to identify such information as confidential and introduce safeguards in internal regulations.

In reference to the non-compete obligation during the period of employment, the best practice is to expressly specify it in a contract, rather than construe it from provisions of the Labour Code on employee's duties. The post-employment non-compete obligation always requires a contractual source.

15.2. The Law of Trade Secrets

Trade secrets (in Polish law referred to as business secrets) are any information which present economic value and are protected by an employer against unauthorized disclosure. The protection of trade secrets can have a form of, e.g., limiting the number of personnel who may become acquainted with them, informing employees who have access to trade secrets about the confidential nature of such information, imposing specific contractual confidentiality obligations on employees who have access to such information. The law does not specify forms of protection of trade secrets. Trade secrets remain confidential even if there is a group of people at the employer, who have access to such information, as long as their number is limited and they are bound by a confidentiality obligation.

Trade secrets may include for example technical, technological or organizational information of the employer, information on internal politics on calculating prices, security measures with respect to commercial data, technical plans, goods and services quality control methods, marketing techniques, organization of work or know-how, results of tests or trials (even if unsuccessful). However, they may not include publicly known information which is legally available to any person.

Under Polish law, former employees (as well as independent contractors/freelancers) are prohibited from disclosing trade secrets of the former employer. Employment contracts (or agreements for termination of employment) may include specific confidentiality obligation of employees, concerning pre- or post-employment period, which supplement the statutory protection of trade secrets. The (former) employee will be released from confidentiality obligation, once information covered by the obligation becomes publicly available or is no longer confidential.

If the employer suffers damage as a result of disclosing trade secrets by the employee, the employer can claim damages under provisions of the Labour Code. Persons responsible for disclosing confidential information may also be criminally liable under provisions of the Criminal Code.

15.3. Restrictive Covenants and Non-compete Agreements

The non-compete obligation may be stipulated during the employment period and/or specific post-termination period of employment. In both cases, the non-compete obligation may have a form of a clause in an employment contract or a separate contract. In any case, such a covenant has to be in writing in order to be valid.

The non-compete obligation (during and after the term of employment) should concern only such activities which can be actually competitive towards the employer, for example selling the same goods or services as the employer. The specific scope should be set out in accordance with the scope of activities of the employer stipulated in, e.g., its articles of association, and actually exercised by the employer. The non-compete obligation should clearly indicate which activities of the employee will be deemed competitive. Generally, employers are entitled to terminate employment upon giving a notice when an employee refuses to conclude a non-competition contract concerning the period during or after employment.

The non-compete obligation during the period of employment can be applied to all employees, whereas the post-employment non-compete obligation can be applied only to key employees who, in the employer's opinion, have access to important information or trade secrets, disclosure of which can cause damage to the employer.

The non-compete obligation concerning the period after termination of employment requires compensation for the entire period of prohibition, amounting to at least 25% of the employee's remuneration for the period of employment just prior to termination, equal in length to the period of the non-compete obligation. In the absence of relevant provision, the former employee can effectively claim statutory compensation in the aforesaid amount. According to the jurisprudence of the Supreme Court, contractual provisions specifying the amount of compensation at a lower level (than statutory compensation) or stating that the employee will not be entitled to it are ineffective. The Labour Code defined its guaranteed amount, which is due to the employee. Moreover, the employee retains the right to compensation even if the employer does not carry out its duty and even if the employee's benefit is no longer relevant to him. This rule is binding and cannot be changed by contractual provisions. It means only that a more far-reaching restriction, which consists of releasing the employer from the obligation to pay compensation before the end of the non-competition agreement, is defective.

The contract remains binding, and a former employee retains his/her claim for compensation irrespective of whether the employer actually pays it or whether the reason for imposing a non-compete obligation no longer exists. The non-competition contract can be terminated earlier only if it provides for such a possibility or both parties agree to earlier termination. The contract may include a contractual penalty, payable by the former employee in case of violation of the non-compete obligation.

15.4. Checklist of Dos and Do Nots

- Specify information considered as trade secrets in a contract.
- Introduce safeguards in internal regulations with respect to trade secrets.
- Put the non-compete contract in writing; otherwise the contract will be invalid.
- Make sure that the post-employment non-compete contract is concluded by a person duly authorized to represent the employer; otherwise the contract will be invalid.
- Set a specific post-employment non-compete period; otherwise, the non-compete obligation will not be binding.
- Insert compensation in the non-compete contract amounting to at least 25% of the employee's remuneration for the period of employment immediately preceding termination, equal in length to the period of the non-compete obligation.
- Pay the contractual compensation without delay; otherwise, the non-compete obligation can be deemed as non-binding on the employee.
- Insert termination clause in the non-compete contract.

16. PROTECTION OF WHISTLE-BLOWING CLAIMS

16.1. Overview

Polish law does not provide for specific regulations on protection of whistle-blowers. In the event of termination of employment, a whistle-blower can challenge the lawfulness of termination before the labour court, according to general provisions of the labour law. Employers often lay off whistle-blowers for reasons not related to reporting (e.g., liquidation of whistle-blower's work post). In such a case, if termination was conducted in accordance with the law, the labour court will not be able to reinstate the whistle-blower.

However, the EU Whistleblowers Directive (*Directive 2019/1937 of the European Parliament and of the Council (EU) of 23 October 2019 on the protection of whistleblowers*), which aims to provide protection to whistle-blowers who report irregularities and violations about which they have obtained information in a work-related context, is to be implemented into the Polish legal order as of December 2021. As of today the provisions of the Directive have not been implemented.

A draft regulation implementing the Directive was published on 18 October 2021. Public consultations were finalized by 17 November 2021, and submitted suggestions are now being processed by the Ministry of Family and Social Policy. At present, it is difficult to predict the exact date the legislator will manage to implement the Directive.

The new whistle-blower protection obligations will, in principle, cover all employers, both private and public sector employers. As an exception, Member States may exempt small employers, i.e., employers with fewer than fifty employees, and so did Poland (according to draft).

The initial draft does not expand the form of protection, since the scope of breaches encompassed by the regulation is identical to the scope provided in Article 2 of the Directive.

The personal scope in the Polish draft seems to be more limited in comparison to the Directive's, as the definition of a 'worker' is based on the Polish Labour Code and the Act on Employment of Part-Time Workers (Article 2 point 12 of the draft regulation) instead of being referenced to the TFEU.

The bill appoints the Ombudsman as the external authority to which whistle-blowers may report breaches.

Throughout the public consultations some non-governmental organizations pointed out possible limitations in the draft regulations, such as:

- the draft bill exempts from protection whistle-blowers that reported breaches of law directly to the press while reserving confidentiality of their personal data due to exempting from the bill's scope regulations on public disclosure; in this case, a whistle-blower reporting directly to the press will fall under protection on the Act on Public Disclosure instead of the act implementing the Directive;
- the draft bill expands the scope of reports excluded from protection to reports breaching professional secrecy, while the Directive mentions that only professional secrecy related to the legal and medical professions may be excluded;

- the draft bill exempts from protection also individuals enjoying immunity from liability or leniency as a result of later cooperation, such as voluntary report of the law violation or cooperation with law enforcement authorities;
- in matters concerning public procurement in areas of national security and defense the regulation is not to be applied;
- the draft bill allows external reports to be submitted via a recorded phone call (a recorded hotline), while the Directive allows both recorded and non-recorded hotlines;
- the draft bill establishes a penalty for untrue reports.

The *vacatio legis* incorporated in the project bill sets an interim period of fourteen days between publication and entry into force.

While introducing internal reporting regulations, employers should make sure that personal data of whistle-blowers is protected from unauthorized access by other employees or third parties. Moreover, reporting by whistle-blowers cannot result in any discrimination, mobbing or other forms of retaliation against them either from other employees or from the employer.

In some cases, employers introduce already internal regulations on reporting by whistle-blowers. Since that can be deemed as an issue concerning relevant changes in the organization of the work, it needs to be consulted with the works council (if any). There is no explicit obligation under Polish law to consult the implementation of reporting regulations with the trade unions (if any). Such requirement may, however, be stipulated in the collective bargaining agreement, provided that there is one applicable to the employer. Even in absence of explicit consultation requirement, it is still advisable to consult implementation of reporting regulations with the company's trade union as reporting by the whistle-blowers is a very significant issue in the scope of employment law matters. The negative result of consultations will not be binding on the employer; however, consultations will show good faith towards the trade union and allow the employer to at least know the trade union's position on the subject and what to expect of them. It should be mentioned that the project bill provides for such consultation obligation with employee representatives.

16.2. Checklist of Dos and Do Nots

- Consult internal reporting regulations with the works council and/or trade unions.
- Include specific protocols in reporting regulations to provide maximum privacy for whistle-blowers.

– Apply security measures to protect personal data of whistle-blowers.

17. PROHIBITION OF DISCRIMINATION IN THE WORKPLACE

17.1. Overview of Anti-discrimination Laws

Anti-discrimination regulations concerning employees (i.e., persons working on the basis of an employment contract) are included in several provisions of the Polish Labour Code. Separate anti-discrimination regulations apply to freelancers, independent contractors, or any other persons who render services under civil law contracts, under the Act of 3 December 2010 on implementing some of the EU regulations in the scope of equal treatment. Anti-discrimination regulations are also included in particular in the Act of 9 July 2003 on hiring temporary employees and the Act of 20 April 2004 on promotion of employment and institutions of the labour market.

Employers need to comply with anti-discrimination provisions stipulated in the Labour Code in all aspects of employment and in reference to all their employees. This includes in particular: commencement, termination and conditions of employment, promotions, access to training for improvement of professional skills, equal pay for the same work or work of the same value.

The Labour Code provides for protection against unequal treatment in particular on the grounds of gender, age, handicap, race, religion and religious denomination, nationality, political views, trade union membership, ethnic origin, sexual orientation, employment on the basis of contract concluded for a definite or indefinite period, full-time or part-time employment (i.e., the qualified criteria).

Unequal treatment can have various forms. The law distinguishes between direct discrimination (i.e., the employee characterized by the qualified criterion is treated less favourably than other employees in a similar situation) or indirect discrimination. The latter always concerns a group of employees characterized by the qualified criteria and not individuals. Indirect discrimination occurs when conditions of employment of such employees are unfavourably disproportionate in comparison to other employees and such disproportion results from seemingly neutral provisions, criteria or actions.

Unequal treatment can also be manifested in particular in refusal to conclude employment or termination of employment, applying penalties or awarding benefits, establishing disadvantageous conditions of employment or remuneration or refusal to promote an employee.

Polish law also defines as forms of discrimination: instigation or ordering other persons to discriminate, harassment (i.e., undesired and unlawful behaviour aimed at or resulting in demeaning or violation of dignity of the employee) and sexual harassment (defined as a form of discrimination relating to gender of the employee).

Not all cases of unequal treatment constitute discrimination. In some situations, employers are entitled to treat employees differently, provided that differences can be objectively justified by valid reasons, such as type or conditions of work, period of employment or work experience. The judicial practice requires discriminated employees to demonstrate the credibility of their claims and reasons for or a qualified criteria of the discrimination. The employer, on the other hand, needs to prove that its actions were not discriminative due to specific objective grounds for treating employees differently, valid under that law. For example, the employer can prove that there was valid objective reason for setting lower remuneration for a male employee and higher remuneration for a female employee, holding the same position, because of greater experience and better qualifications of the female employee.

Under Polish law, employers are generally obliged to prevent and counteract any forms of discrimination, for whatever reason. This includes the obligation to treat employees equally as well as preventing discrimination in relations among employees. Employers are also obliged to make sure that employees have access to a copy of provisions on equal treatment in employment (kept in writing). Employers can keep an extract from relevant provisions of the Labour Code and inform employees where they can access it.

Moreover, according to the Polish Supreme Court decision of 23 October 2019 (case file no. II PK 69/18), the employer has to respect the dignity and other personal rights of employees, to prevent any discrimination in employment, to apply objective and fair criteria for evaluating employees and their performance and to counteract mobbing. The employer's responsibility for the atmosphere among employees is multi-faceted. The duty to influence the shaping of principles of social coexistence concerns not only the relations between the employer and the employees but also mutual relations between the employees. In this respect, the employer should ensure that the employees duly perform their obligation to observe the rules of social coexistence.

In order to be safeguarded against the negative effects of mobbing, an employer has an obligation to introduce an anti-mobbing procedure. The Labour Code does not specify the details of this procedure; however, practice and judicial decisions indicate the following action: introducing the rules of conduct in the event of mobbing, holding regular training, inserting respective clauses to the work rules and carrying out periodical surveys among employees to assess effectiveness of anti-mobbing policy introduced by an employer.

The Polish's Supreme Court rendered a decision of 3 August 2011 (case file no. I PK 35/11) in which it emphasized that preventing bullying at the workplace is an obligation to exercise due diligence. This decision is of significance for employers, as it means that if an employer proves that it undertook real action against bullying (rules, training), it may be absolved from liability. If an employer ignores the obligation to introduce a relevant anti-bullying procedure, then it will be liable even for tolerating negative conduct by its workers or management. It does not matter if the employer knew about the bullying if the employee proves that he/she suffered bullying or that bullying caused their contract of employment to be terminated. In such cases, employees may seek both damages.

If employers violate anti-discrimination provisions in the course of employment, the employee (or a person applying for employment) can claim damages from the employer, amounting to at least the minimum statutory remuneration for work (currently PLN 2,800, ca. EUR 610).

17.2. Age Discrimination

Employees cannot be treated differently because of their age in terms of hiring and layoffs, conditions of remuneration and promotions as well as access to professional training. In the jurisprudence of the Polish Supreme Court, the subject of unequal treatment on the grounds of an employee's age was analysed mainly in relation to termination of employment. Termination of employment solely due to attaining by an employee retirement age is considered age discrimination.

17.3. Race Discrimination

Race discrimination is prohibited under Polish law. Victims of race discrimination have the same rights, generally described in section 17.1 above, as victims of other forms of unequal treatment. In the factual situation of employment relations, the practical aspect of such discrimination remains marginal.

17.4. Sex Discrimination/Sexual Harassment

Sex discrimination is generally understood as unequal treatment of employees due to their gender. This type of discrimination often concerns lower remuneration of female employees, which is not justified by the lower qualifications or experience of such employees. Moreover, in several rulings, the Supreme Court has ruled that termination of employment of a female employee based only on the fact that a female employee attained retirement age constitutes a form of discrimination on the grounds of gender and age.

Under Polish law, sexual harassment constitutes discrimination based on gender. Sexual harassment is displayed in sex-related behaviours towards the employee or in relation to his/her gender. It can have a form of hostile comments or physical actions, a humiliating or threatening atmosphere at the workplace. It is required that such behaviour is undesired by the victim and aimed at or results in violating his/her dignity.

17.5. Handicap and Disability Discrimination

In practice, the most often case of unequal treatment of handicapped and disabled employees is shown by violation by an employer of specific rights and privileges of such employees or treating handicapped and disabled employees less favourably than remaining staff.

Polish law provides for specific regulations concerning employment of the handicapped and disabled, which provide for more beneficial conditions of employment in relation to other groups of employees. Such different treatment of employees is then justified.

17.6. National Origin Discrimination

Unequal treatment of employees based on national origin is prohibited under Polish law and may result in employer's liability under general anti-discrimination provisions. However, this aspect of discrimination is rather rarely debated by the Polish courts. In one of the rulings, the Supreme Court has determined that even though there were differences between remuneration of employees of Polish and German nationality, they were not a sign of national origin discrimination. According to the Supreme Court in that case, the employer was entitled to grant higher remuneration to German employees as they had more professional qualifications. This justifies differences in remuneration.

17.7. Religious Discrimination

Polish law generally protects religious freedom. Any form of religious discrimination is illegal. However, the law explicitly allows applying religious criteria for hiring employees by churches or religious organization of various kinds.

17.8. Military Status Discrimination

Polish law does not expressly mention military status as a qualified criterion of discrimination. However, since under Polish law the catalogue of reasons for unequal treatment is not formally limited, the disadvantageous treatment of employees based on their military status should be deemed illegal, unless the employer can prove that objective reasons existed.

17.9. Pregnancy Discrimination

Pregnancy discrimination is related to gender discrimination. It is often displayed by employers' reluctance to hire pregnant women or young women who may become pregnant. From employers' perspective, hiring such employees can be deemed unprofitable, as they will or may be often absent from work due to maternity leave and other entitlements, and within that period they cannot be laid off. Nevertheless, such actions constitute discrimination.

17.10. Marital Status Discrimination

The marital status is not listed among statutory qualified criteria of discrimination. In practice, employees' claims based on this criterion are rather rare. It should be noted that labour law provides for several entitlements to employees – parents – which are not related to their marital status (e.g., using part of maternity leave by a child's father). If the employer makes exercising of such rights conditional on the marital status of employees – parents – such action could potentially be deemed as discrimination.

17.11. Sexual Orientation Discrimination

Discrimination based on sexual orientation is expressly prohibited under Polish law. In theory, victims of such form of discrimination are entitled to exercise every right under anti-discrimination laws. However, since sexual orientation is considered a private and often an embarrassing issue, claims based on unequal treatment due to sexual orientation are rarely brought before courts.

17.12. Retaliation

Employees who bring a justified legal action against their employer due to violation of anti-discriminative provisions, or in any other way exercise their rights in this respect, are statutorily protected against retaliation from the employer. In particular, exercising such rights cannot be a reason for termination of employment.

17.13. Constructive Discharge

Under Polish law, employers are obliged to prevent any form of discriminative behaviour at the workplace. Employers who fail to comply with this obligation need to consider that employees, who become victims of discrimination, may terminate employment with immediate effect due to gross violation of the employer's basic duties towards the employee and claim for compensation (amounting to remuneration for the period of notice). The employee can also claim damages under general provisions of civil law.

17.14. Checklist Dos and Do Nots

Avoid references to qualified criteria of discrimination while recruiting staff:

- Control remuneration policy to avoid unjustified differences in remuneration of employees.
- Keep a copy (e.g., print out) of anti-discriminative regulations from the Labour Code in a place commonly accessible to every employee and inform employees about it (e.g., in a general e-mail or announcement at the information board).
- Introduce anti-discrimination protocols and make sure that employees follow them.
- Keep a record of any staff decisions which may be related to equal treatment, in particular hiring, layoffs, any changes in conditions of employment and remuneration for a period of at least three years.
- Make sure that drafts of employment contracts and internal regulations do not include any provisions which are discriminative in nature.

18. SMOKING IN THE WORKPLACE

18.1. Overview

Under the Act of 9 November 1995 on protection of health from the consequences of using tobacco and tobacco products, there is a general prohibition of smoking indoors at the workplace, except for smoking rooms. Designating a smoking room is an employer's right, but not an obligation. Therefore, in the event that there are no smoking rooms, employees are not allowed to smoke indoors at the workplace at all. In practice employees often smoke outdoors. Such conduct does not violate the smoking prohibition in the workplace.

If the employer chooses to set up smoking rooms, he/she should comply with the relevant statutory requirements. Smoking rooms need to be designed only for smoking, separated from other rooms and corridors, and equipped with a ventilation system which does not allow cigarette smoke to get to other rooms at the workplace.

There are no regulations concerning smoking breaks in Polish labour law. In principle, employees are obliged to spend their working time effectively working. However, under the Labour Code, employees whose daily working time amounts to at least six hours are entitled to a daily fifteen-minute break within their working time. The law does not limit employees' activities during the break; therefore, employees can use that time for smoking.

According to legal practitioners, if work efficiency is affected by frequent smoking breaks, employers can introduce incentive schemes which would reward increased work efficiency related to employees' abstaining from smoking during working time and breaks.

18.2. Checklist of Dos and Do Nots

– Make sure that the smoking room meets statutory requirements concerning its total separation from other rooms.

19. USE OF DRUGS AND ALCOHOL IN THE WORKPLACE

19.1. Overview

Under the Act of 26 October 1982 on upbringing in sobriety and preventing alcoholism, there is an explicit prohibition of bringing alcoholic beverages to work. Moreover, employers cannot allow intoxicated employees to enter the workplace. In order to verify an employee's condition, the employer can test employees with the assistance of police and trained medical personnel. Tests also need to be conducted if the employee requests them. Under the law, the employer is also obliged to cover the costs of such tests. If, however, tests were requested by the employee and they prove the employee's intoxication, the employee should reimburse their costs to the employer.

In reference to the use of drugs in the workplace, Polish law does not provide employers with tools equally effective as in the case of alcohol. In general, employees do not have an obligation to comply with the request to undergo drug tests. Legal literature suggests that in such cases the employer should draft a record stating the employee's condition and statements of any witnesses to the employee's condition.

In the jurisprudence of the Polish Supreme Court intoxication at work, caused by an employee's fault, is recognized as a valid reason for immediate dismissal of an employee. On the basis of employee's obligations generally stipulated in the Labour Code, a fundamental duty of the employee is defined by jurisprudence and legal scholars as readiness to perform work, i.e., to be able to perform it duly, honestly and efficiently. Therefore, intoxication is understood as a violation of this duty (this can also be applied to intoxication with drugs). Thus, the jurisprudence of the Polish Supreme Court confirms that it is a justified reason for immediate dismissal.

Employers may also include the explicit prohibition of drug and alcohol consumption in internal regulations in order to make employees aware of the gravity of violating this prohibition.

In the event that an employee comes to work intoxicated or drinks alcohol at work, in less significant cases and depending on the employer's approach, the Labour Code provides for the employer's right to impose penalties on the employee, without dismissing him/her. This includes admonition, reprimand or pecuniary penalty (amounting up to employee's daily remuneration for each case of violation). The maximum amount of pecuniary penalties cannot exceed the amount of one-tenth of an employee's remuneration left after deductions allowed under the law. The penalty can be only applied within two weeks since the employer obtained knowledge about the violation, but in any case, no later than three months from the violation.

Provisions of the Labour Code do not allow the employer to request from applicants for a job or from employees information on their drug or alcohol addiction. Such a request can be deemed as a violation of privacy.

According to the jurisprudence of Polish Supreme Court participation of employees in a private occasional or farewell meeting of other employees, organized with the employer's consent and after working hours, in a separate part (social room) of the employer's premises, combined with the consumption of small amounts of alcohol with the employer's consent, does not constitute a serious violation of fundamental labour obligations – unless order and quiet at the workplace or public order were violated.

19.2. Checklist of Dos and Do Nots

- Set out explicit prohibition of consumption of drugs and alcohol in internal regulations and define it as a gross violation of employee's duties.
- In case of an intoxicated employee at work, make sure to have the intoxication confirmed and documented by relevant public services.
- In case of a drugged employee, request the police to conduct a sobriety test.
- If you intend to dismiss the employee who was intoxicated in the workplace, make sure to serve the employee with the dismissal notice within a month after the superior of the employee or person authorized to handle employment matters at the company becomes aware of the employee's intoxication.

20. AIDS, HIV, SARS, BLOOD-BORNE PATHOGENS

20.1. Overview

Polish law does not provide for general regulations concerning obtaining from applicants for job or employees information on Acquired Immunodeficiency Syndrome (AIDS), Human Immunodeficiency Viruses (HIV), Severe Acute Respiratory Syndrome (SARS) or blood-borne pathogens. The Labour Code indicates a specific list of information which employers can collect from applicants and employees. Information about diseases, viruses or other pathogens is not included in that list. Therefore, employers generally do not have a legal basis to request information about AIDS, HIV or SARS from applicants or employees, unless such information is required to assess a person's capability for a given job. Nevertheless, applicants may be vulnerable to such requests from a future employer. They may be motivated to get the job thus willing to provide the employer with any information he/she may request. The law does not include regulations which would practically protect applicants from such enquiries. In reference to the situation of employees, they also do not have an obligation to respond to the employer's questions in this respect. However, their situation is different. According to jurisprudence of the Polish Supreme Court, refusal to respond to questions concerning matters which are not related to the job cannot be deemed as a violation of the employee's duty to comply with the employer's orders. Thus, it cannot justify potential termination of employment.

In specific cases, provisions of the Labour Code justify requesting from applicants or employees information about AIDS, HIV, SARS, other blood-borne pathogens or other diseases. Such request needs to comply with data protection regulations; i.e., it needs to be justified by requirements of the job or its characteristics, e.g., work in healthcare. However, employers may lawfully collect only such information concerning applicants or employees, which is indispensable and adequate for the purposes of performing work at a given position.

Provisions of the Act of 5 December 2008 on preventing and overcoming contagions and contagious diseases in humans are applicable to specific groups of employees. Persons performing work which may involve a risk of transferring contagions or contagious diseases are obliged to undergo specific medical tests, including for AIDS, HIV and SARS. Physicians performing such tests need to provide the employer with a certificate confirming in general if the person is fit to perform given work. Should the result of the tests confirm contamination, the employer, in strict confidentiality, is obliged to move the employee away from performing such work.

It should also be noted that Polish law provides for mandatory medical tests for all groups of employees, such as pre-employment, periodical and control tests. Tests serve as confirmation of an employee's fitness to work at his/her post. If tests confirm the employee's inability to render work at the current position, the employer should move the employee to a different position. If this results in a reduction of employee's remuneration, the employer needs to pay compensatory remuneration for up to six months.

20.2. Checklist of Dos and Do Nots

- Do not ask if the applicant or employee has HIV, AIDS or other diseases unless this information is relevant for a given work.
- Arrange initial and periodical medical tests for employees.
- Move the employee away from work which may involve a risk of transferring an infection or infectious disease, if such action is required on the basis of a medical certificate. Assure confidentially if the change is related to AIDS, HIV or SARS.

21. DRESS AND GROOMING REQUIREMENTS

21.1. Overview

Polish law provides for dress and grooming requirements only in specific respect, i.e., concerning protective wear, workwear, life-saving services or police wear. In the remaining scope, labour law does not regulate these issues.

The provisions of the Labour Code oblige employees to comply with employer's requests regarding employment, which do not violate the law or the employment contract. Therefore, the employer can implement dress code requirements, in the scope related to the performance of work. Relevant requirements can be stipulated in the employment contract, work regulations or other internal documents. According to the views presented in the legal press, dress code requirements should be suited to the job characteristics. They may concern, at the employer's discretion, all employees or just groups of employees such as receptionists, secretaries or employees who have direct contact with the clients. Since the employer is obliged under the Labour Code to respect the dignity and personal interests of employees, dress code requirements cannot be humiliating for employees or violate their dignity; e.g., the employer cannot request employees to wear T-shirts with offensive signs relating to them.

The Labour Code includes regulations related to clothing only with regard to protective wear and workwear. Protective wear is generally defined as clothing which should protect employees during work from hazardous or harmful factors. The workwear is clothing (including footwear) which needs to be supplied by the employer if, in general, the regular garments of the employees may be destroyed or get dirty during work, or if it is necessary due to technological, sanitary or safety considerations. Therefore, relevant Labour Code regulations are applicable to employers whose business involves, e.g., manufacturing or work with hazardous substances.

Under the law, employers cannot allow employees to work without required protective or workwear.

Labour law regulations allow employers to agree with employees to use their own workwear for the performance of specific jobs, designated by the employer. The employer should, however, compensate such employees, considering the prices of relevant workwear.

Requirements regarding protective wear and workwear should be set out by the employer in work regulations unless this was already regulated in a collective bargaining agreement (if any).

According to provisions of the Labour Code, the employer is responsible for keeping protective wear and workwear clean, decontaminated and in a good condition. In reference to workwear, employers may compensate employees for regular washing of their workwear.

Separate regulations concern clothing of the police, security services or life-saving services, etc.

21.2. Checklist of Dos and Do Nots

- Specify dress code requirements in employment contracts or internal regulations.
- Make sure that dress code requirements are suited to job characteristics and that they do not violate employees' dignity and personal interests.
- If there is no collective bargaining agreement, describe requirements related to protective wear and workwear in work regulations.
- Make sure that employees use protective wear and workwear while working. Do not allow employees to commence work without necessary protective wear or workwear.
- Keep protective wear and workwear in a good and useable condition.
- Set a place of keeping protective wear or workwear contaminated with chemicals, radioactive or biologically contagious substances.

22. PRIVACY, TECHNOLOGY AND TRANSFER OF PERSONAL DATA

22.1. Privacy Rights of Employees

22.1.1. Employees' Data

Polish Labour Code allows employers to collect from applicants for a job and from employees the data concerning names and surnames, date of birth, contact data (as indicated by the job candidate or employee), education, professional qualifications and their previous employment if required for a given position. In reference to employees, the employer can additionally request domicile address, PESEL number (namely a personal identification number assigned to each Polish citizen), bank account number (if the employee did not request their remuneration to be paid in cash) and, if that is necessary in connection with exercising by the employee of parenting entitlements, information on another personal data of the employee and names, surnames and birthdates of employee's children. The employer may request documents confirming the accuracy of the data provided by the employee.

Other data may be requested on the basis of explicit statutory authorization (e.g., criminal record from applicants for a job in the police) or employee's consent. However, consent cannot be the basis for processing data concerning the criminal background of the employee. Such data may be processed only if obtaining it is required by law.

In reference to job applicants, according to the views presented by legal scholars, requesting from them personal data other than those listed in the

Labour Code or other statutory provisions, or making the processing of an application dependant on providing such other data discriminates against the applicant and violates his/her dignity and other personal interests.

The consent could be deemed as a valid ground for processing data of an employee or job applicant only if there were no doubts that it was granted freely. Moreover, the consent can concern future data processing only. It cannot legitimize any previous processing commenced without consent or other legal bases.

Lack of consent for processing cannot have any adverse effects on the employee or job candidate. In particular, it cannot be the reason for not employing the given person or terminating the employment relationship with them.

When it comes to processing sensitive data such as racial background, political views, sexual orientation, trade unions membership (any types of data mentioned in Article 9 of the General Data Protection Regulation (GDPR)), processing may be done upon prior employee's consent and only if providing such data was initiated by the employee. Employers cannot ask for the data.

22.1.2. Monitoring of Employees

The issues of employees' privacy and data processing are also related to supervision and control of employees by the employer. The privacy of employees (as well as their dignity and other personal interests) is generally protected under provisions of the Labour Code and the Civil Code. Employers are obliged to respect it. This, however, does not prohibit employers from controlling and supervising employees in the course of performance of work.

Employers are entitled to introduce monitoring (via CCTV or other means) of employees or premises only if it is necessary in order to protect the employer's property or production control or secret information, disclosure of which might expose the employer to the detriment. Video recordings may be kept by the employer for three months. After that time they should be deleted (unless they serve as evidence in legal proceedings). The goals, scope and method of monitoring must be explained in the collective agreement or in the work regulations or in the notice if the employer is not covered by the collective agreement or is not obliged to determine the work regulations. Moreover, the employer is obliged to inform its employees about the planned monitoring at least two weeks before its introduction.

Monitoring of business e-mail box is also legitimate and regulated in the Polish Labour Code according to which employers are entitled to introduce monitoring if it is necessary to ensure the organization of work enabling full use of working time and proper use of work tools made available to the employee. Monitoring of e-mails cannot violate the confidentiality of correspondence and other personal rights of the employee and may concern business e-mails only.

Supervision of employees' activity on the Internet is also subject to the above-mentioned general principles of monitoring.

Employers are not entitled to monitor private phone conversations of employees. However, according to legal scholars and practitioners, employers have legitimate reasons to control business calls of an employee since such calls are made on behalf of the employer and concern his/her business. Hence such form of monitoring is allowed. They can also review phone billings in order to control phone expenses.

The working time of employees working outside the premises of the employer is often controlled by means of Global Positioning System devices installed, e.g., in the company car used by the employee. This form of control is also not regulated in the provisions of the law. According to the views presented in the legal literature on the subject, the employer will be entitled to use such control measures if it is justified by important interests of the employer and provided that the applied means of control are adequate to its purpose. Such form of supervision does not require an employee's consent. Nevertheless, the scope of control needs to be limited. For example, if the employee can use the company car for private purposes, the employer can control the use of the company car only during working time.

Control of the working time by using biometric data, such as fingerprints of employees, has been ruled by the Polish courts as illegal, even in case of prior employees' consent to such form of control and processing of their data. In several rulings, courts have determined that gathering (processing) employees' data – fingerprints, for the purpose of the working time control is disproportionate to that purpose. Registering and controlling the working time can be achieved by other means; therefore, there are no legitimate reasons for the employer to request from employees and process other data than that specified by the law. In such a case the employee's consent cannot be deemed as a sufficient legal basis for data processing, especially that the employee's voluntary consent can be doubtful due to the nature of the relationship between the employer and the employee (employee's subordination). Under the GDPR, processing of biometric data is permissible only upon the employee's consent (and if the provision of such data was initiated by the employee) or if it is necessary for control of access to particularly sensitive information, the disclosure of which may expose the employer to detriment or access to premises requiring special protection.

The searches of employees or their belongings (e.g., bags or purses) by employers are permissible in Poland, although this issue is not explicitly regulated by law. Judgments of the Polish Supreme Court, as well as opinions of legal scholars, confirm employer's right to searches, provided that the search is aimed at preventing and resolving cases of theft at the workplace, or is justified by other important interests of the employer: that it does not violate employee's dignity, its course is regulated by internal regulations of the employer, and employees are aware of a possibility of a search.

According to interpretations provided by the Polish Data Protection Authority, employers can publish names, surnames and job positions of employees on their websites, since all this is official data and it does not relate to employees' private affairs. Employers can also oblige employees to wear badges with their names and name of the company, provided that such obligation is provided for in work regulations. Employee's photo may be published at the employer's website only upon the given employee's written consent.

According to the Polish privacy laws, the personal data of employees can also be entrusted to an external entity (a processor), such as accounting firms for the purpose of keeping personal files of employees and handling other Human resources (HR) matters. The scope of processing needs to be specified in a written agreement, concluded between the employer and the processor.

Polish law requires employers to consult with their works council (if any) all intended actions which may result in significant changes in work organization. This may also include the introduction of monitoring measures, as discussed above. The result of consultations is not binding on the employer. Nevertheless, informing a works council about the implementation of monitoring should take place in advance, before relevant internal regulations become binding. The law does not specify the exact timeframe within which consultation should be conducted, but it needs to be sufficient for the works council to analyse the issue and present its opinion in this respect.

If the relevant monitoring provisions are to be implemented in the work regulations which are in force at the employer, such amendment requires also conducting consultations with trade unions.

22.1.3. Data Transfer

Personal data of employees can be freely transferred to entities which are located in the EU or the EEA Member States, provided that there is a legitimate reason for such data transfer.

In reference to the transfer of personal data outside the EU or the EEA, such transfer is generally allowed if the country to which the transfer is made guarantees the same level of data protection as Polish law. This includes countries recognized by the European Commission as having at least the same standards of personal data protection as required under EU law. Until now, the list of such countries includes in particular: Andorra, Argentina, Canada, Faroe Islands, Guernsey, Israel, the Isle of Man, Japan, Jersey, New Zealand, Switzerland and Uruguay. Transfer of personal data to a country outside the EU or the EEA can also commence on the basis of permission of the Polish Data Protection Authority. Generally, permission may be granted if the data controller (employer) ensures that, in connection with the transfer, rights of the employees are protected similarly as in the EU/EEA. This may be achieved by incorporating, e.g., binding corporate rules and standard contractual clauses into the data transfer contract. The standard contractual clauses are set up in decisions of the European Commission and are recognized as adequate safeguards of personal data. In principle, the Polish Data Protection Authority would not refuse permission for transfer if the contract contains standard contractual clauses.

Alternatively, employers can transfer data on the basis of the employee's consent to the transfer, granted in writing. However, the consent can be revoked at any time. In such a case, employees need to be additionally informed in particular about the purpose of the processing and transfer, risks related thereto, as well as recipients of the data.

According to the GDPR, an employee's personal data may be transferred also in a number of exceptional situations (e.g., the transfer is necessary for the protection of legal claims). However, the employer must always be able to prove that they, in fact, are applicable in the given case.

22.2. Checklist of Dos and Do Nots

- Make sure that obtaining personal data of employees which is not listed in provisions of the law is justified and the data is adequate for the purpose of processing.
- Do not request additional personal data if the purpose of processing can be achieved by using other means.
- Implement specific monitoring protocols and make sure that employees are aware of them (keep records to be able to prove it).
- Apply standard contractual clauses if you cannot determine if a third country provides the same level of personal data protection as Poland.

23. WORKPLACE INVESTIGATIONS FOR COMPLAINTS OF DISCRIMINATION, HARASSMENT, FRAUD, THEFT AND WHISTLE-BLOWING

23.1. Overview

Polish employment law does not provide for specific procedures which need to be applied by employers in order to investigate complaints of discrimination, harassment, fraud, theft and whistle-blowing.

Nevertheless, the Polish Labour Code provides for employer's obligation to prevent mobbing in the workplace, respect the dignity of employees and prohibits any form of discrimination. In order to be able to prove compliance with the aforesaid obligations, in particular concerning the prevention of mobbing, employers in Poland implement internal regulations, such as anti-mobbing procedures or anti-discrimination politics. Employment law does not specify the content of such regulations. However, in practice, regulations usually state that cases of mobbing or discrimination should be reported to an employee specially appointed for that purpose by the employer, or his/her superiors (if the complaint concerns the relevant employee). Regulations usually also provide for an anti-mobbing commission, composed of representative(s) of the employer, representative(s) of employees and a person who does not represent either party (often a psychologist). Composition of the commission should ensure the impartiality and objective assessment of the case. Therefore, persons involved in the alleged mistreatment, in particular possible culprits, should not be appointed as members of the commission. The commission reviews the claims and assesses their validity. The results of the commission's work and its recommendations as to the further course of action are forwarded to the employer. On that basis, the employer commences actions to eliminate irregularities revealed by the commission and to prevent further cases of mistreatment. Usually, employees confirm in writing that they are aware of such internal regulations.

Polish law does not include special regulations with regard to whistle-blowing and investigating complaints. There is only an obligation to have whistle-blowing and ethical procedures and standards that apply to issuers, companies operating a regulated market and entities providing transaction information services.

Under these procedures, the entities will have to ensure that employees who report violations are protected at least against repressive action, discrimination or other forms of unfair treatment.

Directive (EU) 2019/1937 of the European Parliament and of the Council of 23 October 2019 on the protection of persons who report breaches of Union law shall be implemented by the EU Member States until 17

December 2021. Thus, Poland should have implement the above regulations. As of today the Directive has not been implemented. The institutionalized whistle-blower protection at the EU level aims to improve law enforcement and the public interest. In order to prevent and combat corrupt practices and any other illegal activities, the protection of whistle-blowers from retaliation is to be accompanied by the creation of reporting channels. The information on employers obligations in connection with the creation of reporting channels has been specified in section 16.1 above.

The legal practice has developed procedures for handling complaints of employees in respect of irregularities and violations of the law at the workplace. Employers often appoint one or more employees who accept whistle-blowers' complaints on behalf of the employer. Gathering and further processing of the information should be organized in a way protecting the privacy rights of the whistle-blower. Based on the information obtained via this channel, employers may investigate discovered irregularities or violations and remedy them.

The employer should make sure that the course of any such internal investigations is recorded and that documents presented during investigations are kept in the company's files. Such data may become necessary to defend the employer's interests if the employee brings a claim before the court based, e.g., on mobbing suffered at the workplace.

In connection with conducting investigations at the workplace, an employer needs to make sure that in the course of investigation, the dignity of the involved employee is respected. Therefore, persons conducting the investigation, including members of the anti-mobbing commission, need to refrain from making public comments concerning claims of the involved employee, in particular regarding their authenticity. The information obtained during the investigation as well as its course should be kept confidential. Running the investigation should not be entrusted to persons who can potentially be involved in the case under investigation.

Since Polish law does not regulate internal investigations for complaints of discrimination, harassment, fraud, theft or whistle-blowing, there are no explicit statutory requirements for consulting with the trade unions or the works council commencement of such investigations or implementation of investigation regulations. The relevant consultation requirement can be, however, stipulated in the collective bargaining agreement, provided that such agreement applies to the employer, or in existing work regulations. If the investigation regulations are implemented in the form of work regulations, the employer is obliged to consult them with its trade unions (if any), as implementation or changes of work regulations require the involvement of trade unions.

Even in the absence of explicit consultation requirement, it is still advisable to conduct consultations with the trade unions regarding the implementation of investigation regulations since it concerns a very significant issue in the scope of employment law matters.

23.2. Checklist of Dos and Do Nots

- Ensure compliance with the statutory requirements for preventing mobbing or discrimination by implementing relevant internal regulations specifying the course of investigations in this respect.
- Consult relevant investigation regulations with the trade unions.
- Make sure that all employees know investigation regulations and confirm this in writing.
- Keep the record of investigations and relevant documents in the company's files.
- Ensure confidentiality of investigations and protect the privacy of employees involved.

24. AFFIRMATIVE ACTION/NON-DISCRIMINATION REQUIREMENTS

24.1. Overview

The Labour Code provides for a possibility of applying more favourable employment conditions or implementing other measures with regard to certain groups of employees, characterized by age, disability, race, religion/religious denomination, nationality, political views, trade union membership, ethnic origin, sexual orientation, work on the basis of the employment contract concluded for a definite or indefinite period, full-time or part-time employment. The purpose of such actions is to ensure in practical dimension equal chances of all or most of employees having one or more of the aforesaid characteristics if they face underrepresentation, difficulties or discrimination in the labour market or in the course of employment. The period within which such actions apply should be limited.

In practice, affirmative action can have a form of giving priority for hiring candidates belonging to specific groups, e.g., the disabled if their qualifications are the same as qualifications of non-disabled candidates. Such regulations are provided for in provisions on public civil service employees. In cases of professions in which the percentage of female employees is low (and there are no provisions prohibiting women from performing such jobs for example in connection with pregnancy), there may apply incentives for hiring women by giving priority to female employees in terms of hiring or promotions, if they have the same qualifications as men in similar positions.

In general, the law does not regulate or limit the type of measures that can be applied by employers, nor does it provide specific guidelines as to their implementation. Nevertheless, any measures need to comply with the general principles of the labour law. In particular, the employer's action cannot result in violating employees' dignity. It is advisable to outline reasons for taking the affirmative action, relevant group of employees, planned measures and principles of their application in internal regulations. This will help the employer provide reasons for the differentiation of the situation of employees, should such a need arise. According to views presented by legal scholars, measures can be applied to employees but not to job applicants.

It should also be noted that the labour law provides for statutory measures which are intended to ensure protection and equal chances in employment among others in relation to pregnancy, parenthood, age or disability. Statutory regulations provide for protection against termination, favourable conditions of employment or an incentive to hire persons belonging to such groups, e.g., in reference to:

- older persons, namely during the sickness of an employee who is over 50 years old an employer needs to pay 80% of remuneration only during a period of fourteen days in a calendar year, while in the case of other employees this obligation applies for thirty-three days in a calendar year. Upon lapse of the aforesaid periods, sick employees receive payments from the Social Insurance Authority;
- a number of disabled employees at the workplace; employers with a total headcount of at least twenty-five, calculated per full-time positions, are in general released from the obligation to pay contributions to a public rehabilitation fund for the disabled, provided that at least 6% of the total number of employees is disabled.

24.2. Checklist of Dos and Do Nots

- Make sure that reasons for the affirmative action, measures and groups of employees covered by it, as well as its period are stipulated in internal regulations.
- Check whether the situation in the workplace may require the implementation of any measures aimed at making employment conditions equal in relation to specific groups of employees.
- Comply with the mandatory statutory provisions concerning employment in relation to, e.g., pregnancy, parenthood, age or disability.

25. RESOLUTION OF LABOUR, DISCRIMINATION AND EMPLOYMENT DISPUTES: LITIGATION, ARBITRATION, MEDIATION AND CONCILIATION

25.1. Internal Dispute Resolution Process

Employees are generally entitled under the Labour Code to pursue their claims before state labour courts. As an alternative to litigation, the Labour Code provides for a specific procedure which can be applied for resolving employment-related disputes internally. However, it is rarely used as there are usually no competent conciliation commissions appointed at the workplace, and this procedure does not eliminate the risk of commencing litigation by the employee at a later stage. Moreover, the procedure requires the employer's financial involvement. The discussed procedure provides for employees' possibility to request that their claim be heard by a conciliation commission at the workplace, provided that such commission exists at the workplace. The conciliation commissions can be appointed by the employer and by trade unions or with approval of employees (if there are no trade unions). The conciliation commission commences its proceedings upon employees' application (can be filed either in writing or orally).

If the parties reach an agreement, it should be entered in the record of the commission's proceedings and signed by the parties and members of the commission. Even if the agreement has been concluded, an employee is still entitled to claim before a competent labour court that the agreement be found ineffective, provided that he/she believes that it violates his/her relevant interests. Such claim needs to be filed within thirty days from the conclusion of the agreement, and in matters related to termination, expiry or conclusion of employment – within fourteen days.

25.2. Mediation and Conciliation

Under Polish labour law, in case of a dispute, an employer and employee should aim to resolve their quarrel amicably. Very often, employers prefer settling quarrels with the employees in an agreement concluded without involvement of third parties or state courts. This allows them to avoid time- and cost-consuming litigation.

Alternatively, according to provisions of the Polish Civil Procedure Code, parties to the employment relationship can resolve disputes through mediation, provided that a claim can be settled in an agreement (e.g., claim for compensation). Mediation can commence if a mediation agreement has been concluded between the parties (this includes consent for mediation granted upon filing a relevant application by the opponent). Also upon commencement of litigation, the labour court can refer the parties to resolve the dispute through mediation. Each party can at any time withdraw from mediation.

The mediation is conducted outside the state courts system by an impartial mediator (who can be chosen by the parties) listed in a relevant list of mediators.

If the parties reach an agreement through mediation, such an agreement requires approval by the relevant labour court in order to be effective. The court will refuse approval if the agreement violates the law or so-called principles of community life, or aims to circumvent the law or its provisions are unclear or inconsistent.

The course of mediation is confidential and it is often less time-consuming than litigation. If the mediation commences upon referral from the labour court, its period is defined in the court's decision, for up to three months (or longer if both parties agree). If the parties do not reach an agreement within the mediation period, the litigation continues.

The agreement concluded in mediation, upon the court's approval, can be executed in the enforcement proceedings (if its subject is enforceable, e.g., payment of compensation).

In principle costs of the mediation are borne by the parties, based on their agreement. If the mediation commenced upon a referral from the labour court, and it was concluded and approved by the court, parties are released from settling the mediation costs. In case that the agreement was not concluded or approved, and the litigation continues, mediation costs are settled in the final court's ruling.

Despite evident benefits of the mediation, in employment cases in Poland only in a small percentage of cases, the parties agree to that form of settling a dispute.

25.3. Arbitration

The labour law disputes can also be resolved in arbitration. According to provisions of the Polish Civil Procedure Code, arbitration in employment law matters requires the conclusion of an arbitration agreement in writing after the dispute arises. Arbitration clauses in employment contracts concerning future quarrels between the parties are ineffective.

In general, the parties may specify the course of arbitration and arbitrators in the arbitration agreement, or submit the dispute to an existing arbitration court. Arbitration proceeds according to relevant provisions of the Polish Civil Procedure Code, arbitration agreement or procedures of the arbitration court selected by the parties. The proceeding can end with an agreement or award. However, in both cases, approval of a relevant state court is required.

Otherwise, its subject cannot be effectively executed in the enforcement proceedings.

In practice, arbitration is rarely applied in employment-related disputes.

25.4. Litigation

The employment litigation takes place before the divisions of state courts called labour courts. The Polish Civil Procedure Code, also in employment matters, provides for two instances of court. Each party can always appeal against the verdict of the court of the first resort, to the court of the second resort. However, depending on the court of the second resort, effective lodging of an appeal may prove difficult, and appeals may be dismissed at the first hearing. In exceptional cases, parties can lodge an appeal against the judgment of the court of the second resort to the Supreme Court.

The litigation before the Polish state labour courts is usually very time-consuming. Cases usually take more than one hearing to be resolved and between each hearing, there is usually a several-month break. In general claims of employees, resulting from the employment relationship, have a general three years limitation period. In reference to claims related to the termination of employment upon notice, a statement of claims needs to be filed with the labour court within twenty-one days from receiving the notice. In case of immediate dismissal, expiry of employment or refusal of hiring, a statement of claims needs to be filed with the labour court within twenty-one days from receiving relevant information.

If cases concern a ruling stating that the notice of termination was ineffective and the labour court rules in favour of the employee, it can oblige the employer to continue to employ the employee until the ruling rendered in the case becomes final.

Employees' claims often concern remuneration for overtime work, violation of provisions on termination of employment or unjustified termination, desisting from paying severance payments, discrimination (in particular concerning differences in remuneration, or in connection with the commencement of employment) and mobbing.

Disputes concerning discrimination charges can be particularly challenging for employers. This is because, under the Polish Labour Code, the employer needs to provide evidence in its defence and prove that the employee did not suffer discrimination. In the remaining cases, it is the employees who need to prove their claims.

In cases which concern claims of amounts not exceeding PLN 20,000 (ca. EUR 4,444), the Polish Civil Procedure Code provides for a possibility of commencing a simplified proceeding before the labour court. The lawsuit can concern claim(s) resulting from one contract (e.g., from employment contract) and needs to be filed in a special form. This type of proceeding can be often beneficial for employers because the court is not obliged to advise the employee about his potential claims resulting from the given factual situation and cannot recognize in favour of the employee an alternative claim if the original claim was unjustified (as described above). The simplified proceeding should be shorter compared to the regular proceeding, as the court is not obliged to perform several obligations related to the preparation and commencement of the case.

Polish statutory litigation regulations are particularly favourable for employees also in terms of costs of court proceedings. Employees filing lawsuits against employers are generally free of initial and subsequent costs of the proceeding, provided that the value of the subject matter of the case (e.g., amount of the pursued compensation) does not exceed PLN 50,000 (ca. EUR 11,111). Otherwise, there is an obligation to pay a proportional fee of 5% of the value of the case's subject matter; however, the amount of the fee cannot be less than PLN 30 and more than PLN 200,000 (ca. EUR 6.66–EUR 44,444). If the employee lodges an appeal or appeal of the last resort, he/she needs, however, to pay a proportional fee of 5% of the value of the case's subject matter. If the court rules against the employee's claims, it also obliges the employee to reimburse the employer for litigation costs, according to relevant statutory regulations.

Litigation initiated by the employer against the employee generally requires payment by the employer of a proportional fee of 5% calculated from the value of the subject matter of the case (as mentioned above). Once the litigation is completed, the losing party is obliged to reimburse the prevailing party for proceeding costs in accordance with the relevant statutory regulations.

25.5. Fines, Penalties and Damages

Under Polish labour law, fines and penalties are not provided for in employment litigation. Depending on the specific case, employees may claim for reinstatement or damages, the conclusion of an employment agreement or monies due under overtime work regulations.

In general, if the statement of claims concerns termination of employment contract (concluded for an indefinite term) upon notice, which violated relevant provisions of the law, or which was unjustified, the employee can claim reinstatement or compensation equal to his/her two weeks' remuneration up to three months' remuneration. Such compensation cannot be lower than the amount of remuneration due for the employee's notice period. Moreover, if the employee commences work after reinstatement, he/she is entitled to receive remuneration for the time during which he/she was unemployed, in the amount of one month to two months' remuneration (depending on the length of unemployment).

Claims related to the termination of an employment contract concluded for a definite term are limited only to compensation, with the exception of pregnant employees or employees during maternity leave, etc. Compensation amounts to remuneration due for the period of notice.

Generally, in case of termination of employment without notice, which was contrary to the law, employees can claim reinstatement or compensation. The amount of compensation is limited under provisions of the Labour Code and ranges from the amount of remuneration due for the period of notice of a given employee (for contracts concluded for an indefinite term) up to the amount of remuneration equal to the scheduled period of employment but no more than for three months (for contracts concluded for a definite term or contracts for specific work). According to the judgments of the Polish courts, employees dismissed without notice can claim compensation in an amount exceeding the statutory compensation due under the Labour Code, provided that the employee can prove that the damage was suffered to a greater extent.

In case of mobbing or discrimination claims, an employee can seek compensation amounting to at least minimum statutory remuneration (in 2022 amounting to PLN 3,010, ca. EUR 670). Compensation in a higher amount can be awarded provided that damages to a greater extent can be proved.

25.6. Checklist of Dos and Do Nots

- Make sure that the entire process of employment termination complies with the relevant statutory requirements and is well documented.
- Keep the record of proceedings before the conciliation commission and record of any arrangements or settlements made with the employees or former employees outside the court.

26. EMPLOYER RECORD-KEEPING, DATA PROTECTION AND EMPLOYEE ACCESS TO PERSONNEL FILES AND RECORDS

26.1. Overview

Polish employers are obliged under the Labour Code to keep a record of documents relating to the employment of each employee and so-called personal files of employees. The scope of information and documents concerning each employee which employers should keep in files is specified in provisions of law. In case no such records are kept or no protective safeguards are implemented, an employer or a person responsible for that violation (e.g., a manager or a management board member) may be fined from PLN 1,000 to PLN 30,000 (ca. EUR 222–EUR 6,666).

26.2. Personnel Files

According to Polish law, personal files of each employee need to be composed of four parts: 'A', 'B', 'C' and 'D'. Documents in each part of employees' files should be filed in chronological order and numbered, and there should be a full list of documents in each part. Employment law regulations provide for lists of types of documents that should be kept in each part of the files. Part 'A' includes documents which are connected with applying for a job, which can be requested by the employer. Part 'B' covers documents concerning the conclusion of the employment relationship and its course. Part 'C' concerns documents related to the termination of employment. Part 'D' concerns documents related to the disciplinary liability of an employee.

Part 'A' includes documents which are connected with applying for a job, which can be requested by the employer, such as:

- personal questionnaire of a candidate for work submitted during the recruitment process;
- employment certificate issued by previous employer(s);
- documents confirming professional qualifications necessary to perform given work;
- medical certificate (confirming that there are no impediments to working in a specified position), this document needs to be kept in the files, because pre-employment medical examination of employees is mandatory.

Part 'A' may also include documents which the employee can put forward without the employer's request, such as documents confirming a person's skills and professional achievements.

Part 'B' covers documents concerning the conclusion of the employment relationship and its course. These are, for example:

- employment contract and, if the employment contract was not concluded in writing, a confirmation of arrangements as to the type of employment contract and its conditions, as well as scope of tasks (scope of employee's obligations) if the employer has additionally in such a form determined

duties of the employee resulting from the employment contract (relevant documents must be kept in files by all employers);
- certificate confirming completion of OHS training; this document needs to be kept as the employer is obliged to send each employee to such training;
- declaration of an employee who is a parent or legal guardian of a child about his/her intention to exercise his/her rights related to childcare stipulated in the Labour Code, or that s/he does not have such intention, if applicable;
- documents to confirm that the employee was provided with employer's property and is obliged to return it, if applicable;
- documents related to improving professional skills of the employee, if applicable;
- notices of change of conditions of the employment contract or other documents changing those conditions (e.g., agreement regarding change of employment conditions);
- documents connected with granting the employee rewards, distinctions as well as imposing penalties on the employee, if applicable;
- documents concerning granting the employee additional maternity leave, additional maternity leave for an adoptive parent, paternity leave, parental leave or unpaid leave, if applicable;
- documents concerning the reduction of the working time of employees entitled to parental leave, if applicable;
- medical certificates issued in connection with periodical and control examinations, keeping such documents concerns all employers and is mandatory;
- agreement on prohibiting competitive activity during the employment period, if any;
- employees' applications concerning his/her working time system, e.g., on implementing individual working time system, if any;
- correspondence with relevant trade union concerning all matters arising from the employment of a given employee, if any.

Part 'C' concerns documents related to the termination of employment, including:

(1) notice of termination of employment contract or declaration on termination of the employment contract without notice;
(2) documents concerning employee's request for employment certificate and documents related to not paying the employee the pecuniary equivalent for holiday leave;
(3) copy of employment certificate issued to the employee;
(4) confirmation of execution of actions related to garnishing remuneration for work in connection with a court proceeding;

(5) agreement on the prohibition of competitive activity after the employment period (if any);
(6) medical certificate issued in connection with periodical examinations after the termination of the employment relationship.

Part 'D' covers a copy of a notice of punishment and other documents related to the employee's liability to order or liability specified in separate regulations, which provide the removal of the penalty after a certain lapse of time.

Additionally, the employer is obliged to keep other documents which are not part of the employee's files. This includes information on occupational illnesses, accidents at work and benefits paid in connection with these illnesses and accidents. Moreover, the employer must keep for each employee:

- working time register chart, including: work on Sundays and holidays, at night, overtime work and additional days off, as well as duty hours, leave, sick leave and other justified and unjustified days of absence from work, employees applications for time off in connection with overtime work;
- individual chart (list) of paid remuneration for work and other benefits related to work;
- register of workwear or protective wear assigned to the employee, or documents confirming payment of equivalent for using employee's own workwear (if applicable).

26.3. Confidentiality Rules

Employers are obliged to keep personal files confidential and protect them against access of unauthorized persons or theft. In practice, files are usually kept in locked bookcases in locked premises to which access is restricted. The files can be kept electronically as well. Personal files can be accessed only by persons authorized by the employer to work with files. This usually includes HR department employees or accountants. The employer should keep a record of such persons and impose a relevant confidentiality obligation on them. Moreover, the employer is obliged to comply with relevant provisions of data protection law on implementing safeguards to protect the personal data of employees. This includes in particular appointing a person or an external entity as a data protection administrator competent for supervising the compliance of processing and securing that personal data with relevant provisions of law.

If no proper safeguards are in place or the files are accessible to unauthorized parties, the employer (or person responsible at the employer's company, e.g., a manager or a management board member) can be penalized with: a fine (from PLN 1,000 up to PLN 30,000, ca. EUR 222 to EUR 6,666), limitation of freedom, e.g., community service (from one month up to twelve months) or imprisonment (from one month up to two years).

Moreover, employees can claim compensation from the employer under the Polish Civil Code, for damage suffered as a result of inadequate safeguarding of personal files, including not keeping them confidential.

26.4. Employee Access

Under Polish law, an employee (as well as a former employee) is entitled to access his/her personal files. If information in the files is incomplete or false, the employee can request from the employer to correct the errors, attach new documents or remove out-of-date documents (e.g., removing information on reprimand imposed on the employee if the employee has worked during a subsequent twelve months flawlessly). The employee cannot, however, change the content of the files on his/her own. Any changes need to be done by the employer.

27. REQUIRED NOTICES AND POSTINGS

27.1. Overview

Polish labour law provides for employers' obligation to make public announcements to employees in the workplace or provide notices in relation to a number of issues described below.

Provisions on equal treatment

Employers are obliged to make available an excerpt from the provisions of law concerning equal treatment of employees. The excerpt needs to be either distributed in the workplace in writing or made accessible to employees in a manner customary at the workplace. The latter can be achieved, e.g., by way of displaying the excerpt on the information board, or in a different place which is accessible by employees and where it is customary to publish information so that employees know where such information is displayed.

Available job positions

The Labour Code provides for an obligation to inform employees about a possibility of full-time or part-time employment, or employment for an indefinite term (for persons employed on the basis of definite term contracts).

Obligation to make announcements concerns also the holiday leave schedule provided that it is set by the employer. The information needs to be either distributed in the workplace in writing or made accessible to employees in a manner customary at the workplace.

Internal regulations

If the headcount amounts to fifty or more employees, and no collective bargaining agreement applies, employers are obliged to inform employees of remuneration rules and work regulations, as well as any changes to them, at least two weeks prior to their adoption or change. Upon lapse of the two-week period, relevant regulations come into effect. The aforesaid regulations should be announced in a manner customary at the workplace, for example, displayed on the information board or distributed to each employee in writing or in an e-mail. Employers need to make available a copy of work regulations to each new employee before he/she starts work and obtain from such employee a written acknowledgement of receipt and assurance that he/she is aware of its content.

Information on the working time

Employers who hire fewer than fifty employees and who are not covered by a collective bargaining agreement (i.e., employers not obliged to introduce work regulations), the adopted working time system and schedule, as well as adopted working time settlement period need to be announced to the staff. The announcement should be displayed for at least two weeks, in a manner customary for a given employer. Employers need to make available to each new employee before he/she starts work a copy of the aforesaid information concerning the working time, as well as the daily and weekly working time, hours of the night time, manner of confirming arrival and presence at the workplace and justifying absence from work as well as place and date of payment of the remuneration. The employer also needs to obtain a written acknowledgement that the employee received information and is aware of its content.

Collective bargaining agreements

The employer is obliged to notify the staff that the collective bargaining agreements have become binding, changed or terminated. The law does not specify the manner of providing such information. According to legal scholars, the employer can comply with this obligation, for instance, by sending e-mails to employees or display the notification on the information board. Upon specific request of the employee, the employer needs to provide him/her with the wording of the collective bargaining agreement and explain its provisions if necessary.

Appointment of works council

If the average headcount reaches fifty employees, the employer is obliged to display information stating that, because of the number of employees, a works council can be appointed. Information needs to be published according to the practice adopted at the workplace, for example, by putting a notice on an information board.

Work health and safety

Polish labour law stipulates employer's obligation to inform employees about OHS matters, including, in particular: health and life hazards at the workplace, codes of conduct in case of breakdowns or life- or health-threatening emergencies, and preventive measures. Employers also need to inform the staff about employees appointed to provide first aid, prevent fires and conduct evacuations, including their place of work, phone or e-mail. Relevant health and safety provisions require displaying information about employees competent for rendering first aid near the first aid points or kits in the workplace. In the remaining scope, the law does not specify the manner of providing such information; however, the practice indicates that employers can comply with the aforesaid obligations by displaying relevant notices on an information board or distributing it individually to employees. The employer is obliged to make available a copy of the aforesaid information on relevant provisions and principles of OHS to each new employee before he/she starts work and obtain from such employee a written acknowledgement of receipt and assurance that he/she is aware of its content.

27.2. Checklist of Dos and Do Nots

Make sure that work regulations, remuneration rules and collective bargaining agreements are visible and accessible to employees at the workplace so that employees may become familiar with them:

- Distribute or permanently display the excerpt from provisions on equal treatment of employees.
- Keep a record of announcements and information displayed in the workplace to be able to prove compliance with relevant obligations in case of control by the National Labour Inspectorate.

- Keep in employees' files confirmation that new employees were provided with the information on work regulations, working time system, schedule and settlement period as well as information on the provisions and principles of OHS.

www.ingramcontent.com/pod-product-compliance
Ingram Content Group UK Ltd.
Pitfield, Milton Keynes, MK11 3LW, UK
UKHW020148290926
15471UKWH00004B/756

9 789403 503165